I0759800

For Messrs Carter, Blauth, Holmes and Gadeselli, who for years have provided an escape of an altogether different kind.

First published in the UK in 2025
First published in the US in 2025
by Faber & Faber Limited
The Bindery, 51 Hatton Garden
London EC1N 8HN
faber.co.uk

Typeset by Faber in Mr Eaves
This font has been specially chosen to support reading
Printed and bound in Latvia

A CIP record for this book is available from the British Library

ISBN 978–0–571–38294–1

Printed and bound in the EU on FSC® certified paper in line with our continuing commitment to ethical business practices, sustainability and the environment.
For further information see faber.co.uk/environmental-policy

Our authorised representative in the EU for product safety is
Easy Access System Europe, Mustamäe tee 50, 10621 Tallinn, Estonia
gpsr.requests@easproject.com

2 4 6 8 10 9 7 5 3 1

DAVID LONG

Illustrated by
JAMIE COE

GREAT ESCAPES

Inspiring real-life adventures . . .

faber

Contents

Introduction

The Greatest Escapes

From slaves fleeing captivity to wartime heroes and heroines being smuggled across occupied Europe, from dangerous criminals tricking their way out of jail to ordinary men and women who got caught in the wrong place at the wrong time . . . The best escape stories combine as much excitement, ingenuity, courage and luck as any fictional adventure, but they are far more inspiring.

Many of the most daring escapes have involved prisoners of war. For them, digging a tunnel or climbing a high wire fence was just the start. The real challenge was travelling hundreds or sometimes even thousands of kilometres through enemy territory to reach freedom. Most couldn't speak the local language, and many lacked a map to help them navigate a safe route through countries they had never seen before. It's no wonder that of the hundreds of thousands who were taken prisoner during two world wars, less than 1 per cent escaped and made it home.

But, of course, not all escapees are military heroes. The stories of slaves risking their lives to save themselves and their families are even more amazing, but what about the ordinary criminals who escaped from jail and then spent years on the run? Their lives were hardly heroic, but in a few famous cases they, too, showed extraordinary cunning and imagination – and a handful of them have never been seen again.

Great Escapes tells the true stories of the good and the bad, the lucky successes as well as the occasional failures.

Henry 'Box' Brown

The Crate Escape (US, 1849)

America was home to around four million slaves in the mid-nineteenth century, when an especially cruel law meant that any children born to a slave automatically became slaves themselves. One of them was Henry 'Box' Brown, who spent thirty-three years as a slave in a state called Virginia.

Many of the slaves were beaten, starved and abused, but Brown's owner was quite a kind man and the two got on well. As a teenager, Brown was allowed to earn some money of his own working in a tobacco factory, and later he started a family after meeting another slave called Nancy and falling in love.

Nancy's owner agreed not to sell her or any of their three children, as long as Brown paid him a certain sum of money each week. Brown would pay on time, but then the man suddenly changed his mind and Nancy and the children were taken away. Brown was devastated by this betrayal

and heartbroken at the loss of his family, so he made up his mind to escape from Virginia as soon as he could. He decided the best thing to do was to head for the city of Philadelphia, which was nearly 400 kilometres away. Slavery existed there too, but campaigners were working hard to put an end to it. Brown had heard of an organisation in the city that helped slaves just like him. The Pennsylvania Anti-Slavery Society's members were known as abolitionists, and they wanted to see slavery banned across America, just as it had been in Britain a few years earlier.

Unsurprisingly, African Americans like Brown were forbidden by law from just jumping on a train or hitching a ride out of town. Brown knew that even his owner wouldn't allow a valuable slave simply to run off, so he had to devise a cunning escape plan. Before long, he had an idea that he hoped would enable him to escape without anyone noticing he was gone until he was safely out of Virginia.

Brown had managed to save more than a hundred dollars by working hard at the factory, and he persuaded a couple of men to help him put his plan into action. Both were called Smith, but they were not related to each other. James Smith had been a slave himself but was now free, while Samuel Smith was a bootmaker, a white man who felt sorry for Brown after hearing how his young family had been stolen from him. Both men knew they would be taking a big risk, because helping a slave escape was a serious crime in Virginia.

Brown explained his idea to his friends, describing how he wanted them to lock him in a large wooden box or crate and then send it to Pennsylvania using a delivery company called

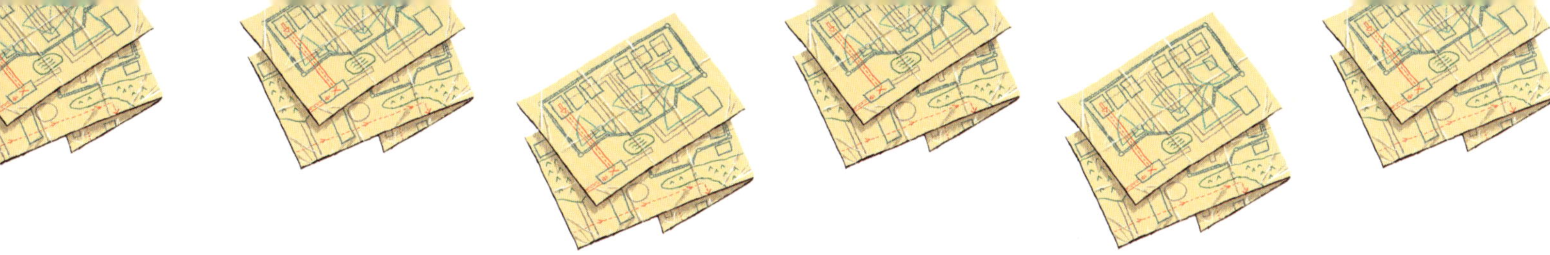

Adam Express. The company had a good reputation for carrying heavy parcels and other cargo. It charged a fee for this service, based on the size and weight of whatever it was being asked to carry. This is why Brown had needed to put aside so much money before attempting his escape.

The plan sounded simple enough, but Brown needed a lot of luck for it to succeed. He had a sharp tool called an awl that could be used to make breathing holes in the box, and he planned to take some water with him for the journey. However, even with these precautions there was a good chance that something could go wrong. If Brown made even the slightest noise while he was in the box, he might be discovered by someone at Adam Express and get sent back to his owner. If that happened, he was sure to be whipped or viciously beaten, but even if he wasn't discovered, he risked being seriously injured if the box was accidentally dropped. He could even die inside it if the delivery was delayed for some reason or the box was put on the wrong wagon and ended up making a much longer journey to a different location.

However, Brown was desperate and so determined to escape that he didn't mind taking these risks. He asked Samuel Smith to travel to Philadelphia first and contact the members of the Pennsylvania Anti-Slavery Society. He wanted Smith to explain to them what was going on, in the hope that its members would help him. Luckily, as soon as Smith told the Society about the disappearance of Brown's family and the effect this had had on him, they agreed.

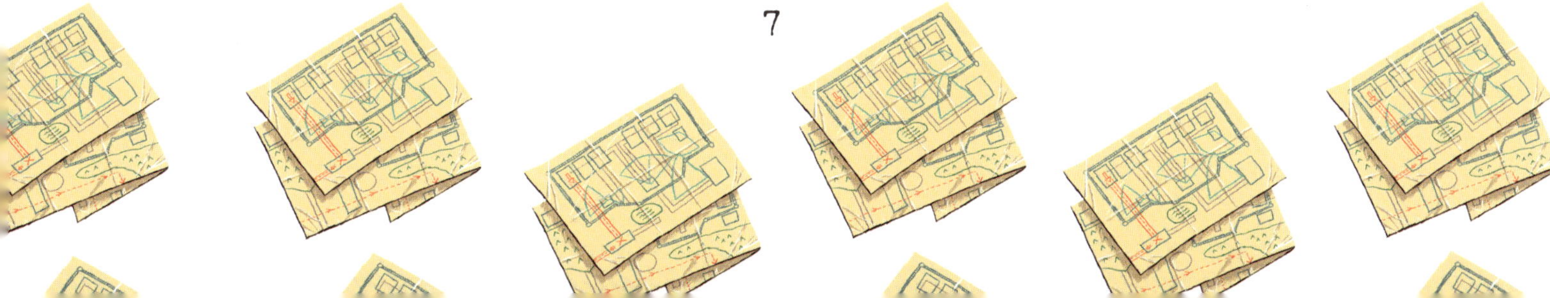

Smith was instructed to address the box and its contents to a local businessman called Passmore Williamson. Williamson had a young family just like Brown and wanted to help. Even before climbing into the box, however, Brown had to think of a way to slip away without his owner immediately noticing that he had gone. Obviously, if he didn't turn up for work on time, his disappearance would be reported, but if he could stop this happening straightaway, it would give him time to cross the border out of Virginia. Once he'd left the state, it would be much harder for anyone to bring him back.

The way Brown planned to do this was clever, but gruesome. One morning in March 1849, he deliberately burned one of his hands with concentrated sulphuric acid. This scorched the skin down to the bone, and the wound looked really terrible. The pain must have been horrific, but it meant Brown could have a day off work. This gave him the chance he had been waiting for. Later that day, he climbed into a wooden crate, with some water and a few dry biscuits to nibble on. As he was about 1.7 metres tall, this meant having to carefully fold himself into a space less than a metre long and only 60 centimetres wide and 75 centimetres high. The lid was then firmly nailed down by his friends and the crate loaded on to a cart belonging to Adam Express. There was no turning back.

The journey to Philadelphia was uncomfortable, and it lasted all night and most of the next day. For more than twenty-seven hours Brown felt himself being bumped and bruised as the box was lifted from the cart and into a railway wagon, then on to a boat, into another

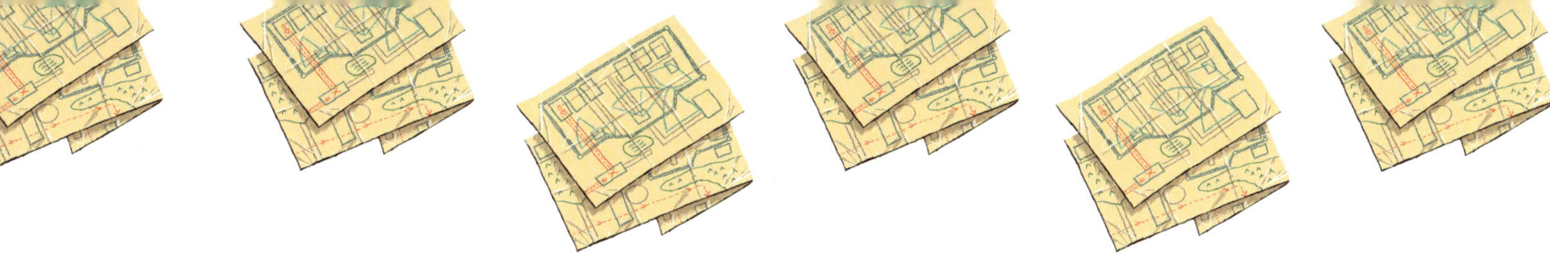

wagon, on to a river ferry, then another train, and finally on to another cart, which took it to Passmore Williamson's office.

There were clear instructions on the crate that read 'HANDLE WITH CARE' and 'THIS WAY UP', but Brown was dropped several times, and more than once he found himself stuck upside down. This was extremely uncomfortable, but he could breathe and somehow he managed to remain still and silent the whole time. In this way he managed to avoid detection, until eventually he heard the nails being prised from the lid. Moments later, enormously grateful, he found himself standing in a room surrounded by the relieved, smiling faces of the Philadelphia abolitionists.

Brown's ordeal earned him the nickname 'Box', and the escape turned out to be the first of several involving Williamson and his abolitionist friends in the Society. Sadly, Brown himself was never reunited with his family and, after writing a book about his escape, he realised he had made it almost impossible for anyone else to copy him. Once slave owners heard how Brown had got away, they'd take steps to stop their own slaves doing the same. However, a stage show based on this extraordinary escape made Brown a celebrity, and he was able to put his fame to good use, highlighting the evils of slavery not just in America, but also around the world.

Harriet Tubman

Riding the Underground Railroad (US, 1849)

The Underground Railroad was the name given to a network of small, secret organisations that existed in America from the 1830s to the 1860s. Its members were volunteers known as 'conductors', and they helped an estimated 70,000 African Americans escape from slavery. Most wanted to get away from places like Kentucky, Virginia and Maryland (where slavery was still a part of everyday life for thousands of men, women and children) in order to reach towns and cities where they could live freely.

Harriet Tubman was one of the most famous. Both her parents were slaves, so she'd become a slave the day she was born. This was probably in Maryland in around 1820, although, like most slaves, Tubman never had any official documents proving when or where she was born. Work began when she was only five or six years old, which wasn't unusual for a slave. Her job involved caring for a baby. One of her tasks was to rock its cradle for hours and hours, and she was beaten whenever the baby cried or if it woke up at the wrong time. Once, Tubman was whipped so badly by the baby's parents that she was

scarred for life. From then on, she began wearing extra layers of clothes to give herself a bit of protection.

Once the young girl grew taller and stronger, she was ordered outdoors to do heavier farm work. This usually involved ploughing fields and hauling logs from the forest, but by the time she was a teenager she was being sent further out to the marshes that surrounded the farm. Here, she was responsible for trapping muskrats, enormous rodents that can damage crops if they are not kept under control.

Muskrats have a ferocious bite, but even out in the marshes the real danger for Tubman still came from other humans. She was often beaten and told she wasn't working hard enough. Once, she was struck hard on the head by a large metal object thrown by one of the men responsible for guarding the slaves. The blow left her bleeding and unconscious for two days. It probably also fractured her skull, although we can't be sure about this because no one thought it was worth calling a doctor 'just' to examine a slave.

Tubman never fully recovered from this injury. It still affected her ability to work when she was in her twenties, so her owner decided to get rid of her. Tubman felt sick at the idea of being sold to someone else, even though her owner was violent and cruel. She decided she would rather be free or even dead than sold like a farm animal, so, in September 1849, she made up her mind to run away.

The first attempt failed when Tubman's owner offered a $100 reward to anyone who brought her back. $100 was about a month's wages for most people (which shows how valuable slaves were in America), and the prize helped ensure Tubman was soon detained. However she refused to be defeated and tried again a few weeks later, this time with help from the Underground Railroad.

Many of the conductors on the Railroad were ex-slaves themselves; others were just ordinary Americans – farmers, teachers and shopkeepers who were appalled by the cruel treatment of slaves and wanted them to enjoy the same rights as everyone else in the country. Religious groups also got involved, especially those affiliated to the Society of Friends (who are also known as the Quakers). Being part of the network could be almost as hazardous for the conductors as it was for the slaves. Helping a slave escape was a criminal offence in many states. One volunteer was jailed for six years; another was sent to prison for a year and had the letters 'SS' (for 'slave stealer') burned into his hand. Armed men known as bounty hunters were a constant threat. They made a living by catching escaped slaves and often became violent if anyone tried to stop them returning these captives to their owners.

Because of this, everyone who had anything to do with the Railroad kept very quiet about it, so Tubman did too. Even after she was free she refused to say how she'd got away and wouldn't describe the help she'd received. This was so that other slaves could use the same

route as she had and avoid being caught. What we do know is that she trekked nearly 250 kilometres to get away from her owner, which she did on foot because slaves had no alternative. Tubman and her fellow runaways also had to move around at night, using the stars to navigate and hoping they weren't spotted by a bounty hunter or anyone likely to report that they had seen a black person behaving suspiciously.

The Railroad conductors occasionally used their own money to buy whole families of slaves so that they could set them free. But mostly they helped by providing runaways with food and drink, or by finding places where they could stop and rest. Usually this meant in the volunteer's own home, although it was important to make it look as though the 'guest' was an ordinary, hard-working slave. In nineteenth-century America, most white people didn't have black people over to stay, and if such a person was spotted by a nosy neighbour, he or she would almost certainly be reported to the authorities. For the same reason, people on the run sometimes carried tools when they were passing through a strange town or city. That way it would look as though they were simply on their way to work.

Fortunately, by hiding out during the day Tubman managed to reach Pennsylvania without being caught. This was a much safer place for an ex-slave than Maryland, but when a new law was passed a few months after her arrival, it changed everything. The ruling meant that the police (who in America were called sheriffs and deputies) could now arrest runaway

slaves even in areas where slavery had been abolished. This terrible law was called the Fugitive Slave Act, and it threatened the lives and freedom of everyone who had managed to escape using the Railroad. As a result, beginning in 1850 many ex-slaves fled to Canada. If they stayed in America, they risked being recaptured and sent back to their old owners, who, they knew, would punish them severely.

Tubman could have fled north too and gone on to enjoy a safe, peaceful life in Canada. Instead, she decided to become a conductor herself and, although she did go to Canada, it was only because she guided a group of eleven escaped slaves to freedom there. Once again, this involved moving around only after dark and walking an incredible 700 kilometres without being spotted and arrested.

Tubman quickly proved herself to be as tough as she was determined, and on a later trip north she actually threatened to shoot a member of her group who was so exhausted he wanted to turn back. Doing so would have endangered everyone else, so Tubman just growled, 'You'll be free or you'll die,' and then ordered everyone to quieten down and keep on walking.

In all, Tubman is known to have rescued around seventy people. This involved her going back to Maryland at least a dozen times on her own, which was incredibly courageous for someone who knew she would be arrested immediately if she was caught. She even carried on after enraged local slave owners announced they were offering an enormous

$40,000 reward to any bounty hunter who could catch or kill her before she freed any more slaves.

Happily, no one was able to, and Tubman made it home safely every time. When slavery was finally abolished in America in 1865, she worked hard to open a home for freed slaves who were too old and poor to look after themselves. Even in her nineties she refused to slow down. She joined the campaign to win the right for women to vote in American elections and is now regarded as a heroine for her bravery and determination.

Winston Churchill

The Ghost in a Coalmine (South Africa, 1899)

Sir Winston Churchill is mostly remembered today for his time as Britain's prime minister during World War II. He made many inspiring speeches designed to keep the public's spirits high at a time when German bombers were attacking British cities every night and it looked as though the country might actually be defeated.

Even Churchill's enemies agreed that he was very good with words. This was perhaps not surprising as he had been a talented and highly successful journalist long before he went into politics. His name had first hit the headlines more than forty years earlier, when he travelled to South Africa and worked as a newspaper reporter covering the fiercely fought Boer War (1899–1902). The conflict involved mostly British troops against Dutch and German settlers known as Boers who had taken over this part of the continent. The fighting was brutal and thousands were killed on both sides, including many civilians. Inevitably, this made the job of a war reporter even more hazardous than usual, but the twenty-five-year-old Churchill didn't mind this at all. He had trained as an army officer and clearly enjoyed danger and excitement.

Unfortunately, Churchill's enjoyment didn't last very long, because he was captured by the Boers on 15 November 1899, barely two weeks after his arrival. It happened after he had stopped to help rescue around twenty British soldiers who had been wounded during a savage attack on a military train. Churchill and several other prisoners were then marched for two days across country before being put on a second train, which chugged slowly along for another twenty-four hours. When it reached its destination, they were taken off and locked in a school building that had recently been turned into a prison.

The enthusiastic young reporter was convinced that he would be released shortly, but he was wrong. Although he had documents proving he was a journalist, and had been unarmed at the time of his arrest, the Boers refused to believe his story. Instead, Piet Joubert, one of their most senior army generals, filed a report saying that Churchill was so dangerous that he ought not to be released until the end of the war.

Churchill was furious about this and extremely bored by his new prison routine. After just a few weeks he made up his mind to escape and with a couple of other prisoners began looking for ways to get out. The prison was well guarded, but he managed to persuade his companions that they could sneak over a section of its main wall without being seen. The best place to do this, he said, was by the outdoor toilets, where a brick ledge on the wall provided a perfect foothold that would enable them to clamber over.

Churchill wanted to put his theory to the test as soon as he could, and on 12 December he managed to climb over the wall and drop down to the other side without anyone seeing him. Hiding in a bush, he waited for the other two to join him, as agreed, but neither did. In fact, both of them had been surprised by one of the sentries and ordered back into the school building at gunpoint. Luckily, it hadn't occurred to the guard that a third prisoner might already have gone over the wall, but this left Churchill in a very difficult position. He was now completely alone, without any money or a local map or even a compass. Also, he couldn't speak the local language, which would be a problem if he was stopped while trying to cross the Transvaal, the vast area occupied by the Boers, on foot. Reaching safety would mean Churchill hiking almost 500 kilometres through enemy territory. The idea of doing this on his own was so daunting that he briefly considered climbing back over the prison wall and giving himself up.

He could think of one alternative, however. If he could get to the railway line, it might be possible to sneak on to a freight train. The right one would take him safely out of the Transvaal to Lourenço Marques, a coastal city (now called Maputo) in the Portuguese colony of Mozambique. But getting on to a train was far from easy. There were more guards posted between the prison and the railway line, and as Churchill crawled out of his hiding place in the bushes he narrowly missed bumping into one of them, who was standing only a couple of metres away.

Even after getting away without being seen and disguising himself by stealing ordinary clothes to replace his prison uniform, Churchill realised that he would attract attention if he was spotted hanging around the station. Because of this he decided the safest place to board a train was about 200 metres outside the station, where the line curved sharply. This, along with a slight uphill gradient, meant train drivers had to slow down, which would make it easier for Churchill to leap into one of the goods wagons, hopefully without the driver or anyone else seeing what he was up to.

This part of the plan worked perfectly, and some empty coal sacks that had been stored in the wagon meant he was reasonably comfortable for the first 100 kilometres or so. However, once the sun came up, Churchill began to worry about being seen, so he decided to jump down from the wagon and made his way towards an isolated house, desperately hoping that whoever lived there might be friendly and helpful.

To Churchill's horror, he was greeted at the door by a man with a gun. The weapon was pointed right at him, and the man holding it gruffly asked him to identify himself. Churchill knew he couldn't disguise his English accent, but he pretended he was a doctor and said he had got lost after falling off a train. This didn't sound at all convincing, and the man gestured for Churchill to get inside by waving the gun in his face. Churchill suddenly lost his cool and blurted out his real name. When the man heard this, he smiled broadly and, to Churchill's enormous relief, put the gun down. He said the Boer police were looking everywhere for the escaped prisoner, and managed to persuade Churchill that his own house would be a safe place to hide out.

The Boers were determined to get the Englishman back and had offered a large reward for information leading to his arrest. Because of this it was decided to hide Churchill in a nearby coalmine. Obviously he couldn't refuse this offer, but conditions underground were so bad they made the prison in the old school building seem like a luxury hotel. The mine was cold, dirty, dark, damp and rat-infested. For once in his life Churchill was far too uncomfortable to be bored.

He managed to endure the discomfort for three full days, during which one mineworker spotted him and ran away, thinking he had seen a ghost. The next day Churchill was smuggled on to another goods train, together with a bag containing a couple of cold roast chickens, a melon, a loaf of bread and three bottles of warm tea. It was a long journey to the coast, at least 400 kilometres, so he hid among some bales of wool and made himself as comfortable as he could.

Once again the train was agonisingly slow, but at least this one was heading to safety. At one point it actually stopped and then remained stationary for nearly eighteen hours. To his horror, Churchill heard some men approaching during this agonising wait, and for a couple of minutes he could feel one of them poking around among the bales of wool. Clearly, a search was under way, but luckily the man was too lazy or incompetent to do the job properly.

Churchill's heart must have been thumping wildly, but eventually the wagon lurched forward and the train began to gather speed. Each time it slowed as it rolled into a station, he peered out from his hiding place at the name painted above the platform. As soon as he spotted a sign written in Portuguese, he jumped out, knowing he must be over the border. The Boers were safely behind him now, and Britain's future prime minister was free at last.

Gunther Plüschow

The Only German to Make It Home (China, 1914)

Enormous numbers of men, women and even children were captured by enemy forces during the twentieth century's two world wars. Both sides in these conflicts established hundreds of their own prison-of-war camps, and at least 20 million men and women (known as POWs) were locked up in them, often for years at a time.

Soldiers, sailors and airmen often felt they had a duty to escape, and some tried again and again. Many of their attempts were brave and imaginative, but hardly any were successful. Most of those who escaped were quickly recaptured, and only a very few made it home before the fighting was over. Of those who were successful, just one was German, and his name was Gunther Plüschow.

Even POWs who were able to find a way out of a prison camp without being seen faced all sorts of difficulties once they were on the run. Their prison clothing often gave them away, and at this time hardly anyone spoke a language other than their own, which made them stand out even more. Also, prison camps were often built in remote areas, and navigating through unknown countryside was almost impossible without a map – which POWs were forbidden to possess. Something else they didn't have was money for food. Unless they could find somebody local to help them (which didn't happen very often in wartime), most had no choice but to walk enormous distances, while sleeping out in the open, eating whatever food they could steal and hoping for the best.

When Gunther Plüschow began his escape he wasn't a prisoner of war, but he faced many of the same problems. He was a navy pilot who had been assigned to a small force in China, where Germany was trying to establish an Asian empire. His job was to fly one of two military aircraft that had been sent by sea from Germany. Unfortunately, these were fragile and old-fashioned, and one of them crashed, killing the pilot, shortly after taking off for the first time.

In August 1914, at the start of World War I, this part of China was invaded by the Japanese army and the Germans retreated. Plüschow was given the important task of flying a stash of top-secret documents out of the country, but he didn't get very far before crash-landing in a rice field. Although the machine was badly damaged, Plüschow was uninjured. He set fire to the wrecked aircraft so the Japanese couldn't repair it and then left the area on foot. His plan was to get to the port of Shanghai, where he hoped to board a ship back to his homeland.

Germany was more than 8,000 kilometres away, but Plüschow was fortunate enough to have some money. He paid to travel part of the way to Shanghai on a riverboat called a junk and then bribed a railway guard to let him board a train. Unfortunately, by the time it reached the city, fierce fighting across much of Europe meant no more ships were going to Germany.

Plüschow appeared to be stranded, but then, in an incredible stroke of luck, he ran into an old friend, who offered him a fake passport. This document made it look as though he was Swiss, not German, and called Ernst Suse. This was very helpful because Switzerland was a neutral country, which meant it wasn't fighting on either side in the war. If people thought the runaway pilot was Swiss, he was much less likely to be arrested on his way back to Germany.

Plüschow still felt on edge. He was convinced the Shanghai police thought he was a spy and were watching him wherever he went. To avoid arrest, Plüschow hurried down to the port as fast as he could and used his new Swiss passport to board the first foreign ship he could find. The vessel was an American one, and it got him out of China – but it was heading straight for Japan! Plüschow's only hope now was that no one would notice that his passport was a forgery when the ship reached Japan. To his surprise, nobody did, and he must have breathed a huge sigh of relief when the ship then left Japanese waters and began making its way slowly across the Pacific Ocean.

The next stop was San Francisco, on America's west coast, where Plüschow left the ship. America was also neutral, and he felt certain that if he could catch a train to New York, he would finally be able to find a ship bound for Europe. He knew he still had to be very careful, though. America wasn't at war with Germany, but it had very strict laws about foreigners carrying fake passports and using false names.

Incredibly, his luck held out once again. New York was on the other side of the country, nearly 4,500 kilometres away, but he managed to get there without anyone suspecting who he really was. At the harbour he found a ship that was sailing to Europe, so he bought a ticket and rushed aboard.

This final part of his voyage should have taken him just four days, even in wartime, but the ship made a sudden, unscheduled stop in Gibraltar. Now Plüschow knew his luck really had run out. Gibraltar is the only British port in the Mediterranean, and there were soldiers and sailors everywhere he looked. One of the officers spotted Plüschow almost immediately and became suspicious. Plüschow was promptly arrested, locked in a cell and then put on the first available ship bound for England.

Plüschow had been on the run for almost ten months. In that time he had travelled more than halfway round the world, but now he found himself stuck behind a three-metre barbed-wire fence somewhere deep in the English countryside. The fence surrounded a POW camp in the grounds of an old country house called Donington Hall, and Plüschow didn't like being there at all.

Within weeks he had made up his mind to escape, and one night, during a heavy thunderstorm, he and another German called Oskar Trefftz helped each other over the fence. This wasn't that difficult as POW camps in England were often very poorly guarded, probably because the authorities felt that escaping from an island is so difficult that most prisoners wouldn't bother trying. This pair were determined, however, and thought they would stand a better chance if they split up. Trefftz was quickly caught and returned to the camp, but Plüschow managed to reach London by train without being detected. When he arrived he cheekily spent several hours exploring the British Museum like an ordinary tourist.

Newspapers soon began to report the escape, however, and one of them described the prisoner's blond hair, his smart appearance and even a dragon tattoo he got while he was in China. Plüschow realised he needed to disappear again as soon as possible. This time he decided to trek east along one bank of the River Thames, but only after disguising himself by blackening his hair with shoe polish and soot. He hoped that rubbing some more soot into his clothes would make them appear old and worn-out.

Clearly, the only way he could leave England was by sea, but both banks of the Thames were swarming with police and military personnel. Plüschow knew he would be arrested if he tried to board a ship in the normal way, and for a while he had no idea what to do. He spent several nights sleeping rough in a park in Kent, but then spotted a Dutch ship that looked

like it was preparing to sail. It was moored on the far side of the river, which was annoying, but Plüschow thought he would be able to sneak on board if he could find a way to cross the water.

It was cold and much too far to swim, but he came upon a solution later the same day, when a young couple rowed across the river in a small boat. They soon wandered off, and Plüschow waited until they were out of sight before jumping into their boat and rowing as fast as he could over to the other bank. Once he was alongside the Dutch ship it took him only a minute to climb up its slippery anchor chain, and another minute to find a hiding place beneath the canvas cover of one of the lifeboats.

Luckily, no one had seen him do this, and a few hours later the ship docked at the port of Vlissingen in the Netherlands. As that country was also neutral, the rest of Plüschow's journey was as straightforward as it would be now. Hilariously, when the exhausted globetrotter finally reached Germany, he was accused of being a British spy, but once he had identified himself and described his remarkable journey he was welcomed home as a hero.

More than a century later, Gunter Plüschow is still famous as the only German who managed to escape from Britain in either of the two world wars.

Eliza Maud Inglis

Refusing to Sit Still (Russia, 1917)

Eliza Maud Inglis was born in the remote hills of northern India. She moved to Britain as a teenager in 1878 and went on to become one of the first women in Scotland to qualify as a surgeon.

Inglis was a humanitarian and a passionate feminist too. As Scottish medical schools refused to admit female students, she helped establish a new one for them in Edinburgh. She was also a strong supporter of votes for women and during World War I raised the equivalent of £50 million to set up and run more than a dozen battlefield hospitals in various countries around Europe. These were staffed by 1,500 volunteer doctors and nurses, mostly women like her, from Scotland, Canada, Australia and New Zealand.

Elsie, as her friends called her, had planned to open only one hospital at first, to help the Red Cross and the Royal Army Medical Corps treat the terrible injuries that were being inflicted on enormous numbers of soldiers. However, much like the medical schools a few years earlier, neither organisation wanted anything to do with her. Both seemed to think there was no place on the battlefield for women, even for those who were highly qualified doctors and nurses. Inglis strongly disagreed with this notion and became determined to prove them wrong after being told by one official to 'go home and sit still'.

To begin with, only the French government was interested in her generous offer, possibly because its soldiers were being killed and injured in even greater numbers than British ones. In 1915 Inglis opened a brand-new, hundred-bed hospital for them, but as the fighting worsened it was quickly expanded to treat several hundred patients at a time. Despite the endless demands of her medical work, she still found time to design a special grey uniform for the staff. This included tartan fabric as a reminder of her native Scotland.

Once the hospital was working well, she went to Serbia, a tiny country in central Europe that, like France, was being torn apart by the war. Tens of thousands of Serbians had been killed and wounded in battle, and thousands more were dying of typhus. This is a disease spread by insects called lice, which live on people's skin and in their clothes. They thrive in the filthy conditions of wartime, and over a period of six months a deadly typhus epidemic killed more than 200,000 Serbian men, women and children out of a population of only three million, with some 30,000 prisoners of war also dying. Inglis was horrified by these numbers, so she rushed to open another four hospitals to treat the disease. Conditions there were far better than in the military hospitals, and the infection rate fell steeply. This made

Inglis enormously popular in Serbia, but working in the clinics was extremely dangerous for her and her staff. Several nurses caught typhus and died, and in October 1915 dozens more were captured and held at gunpoint when Serbia was invaded by the Austrian and German armies. When more enemy troops took over the hospital in Kragujevac, their prisoners included its chief medical officer, Inglis herself. It took until the next year for any of them to be released and allowed to travel back to Britain.

Inglis had become seriously ill by this time, and she probably realised that her symptoms meant she had cancer. She knew she should rest but refused to slow down, and as soon as she reached Scotland she began fundraising again. This time the money was needed for a hospital in Russia, because many Serbian troops had gone there following the invasion of their small country.

Inglis went to join them a few months later, taking 50 tonnes of medical equipment with her and more than a hundred new volunteers. Soon these women were busy treating hundreds more wounded every week, but in Russia the danger came from two directions instead of only one. The main threat was still the German army, which was getting closer and closer. Several times Inglis and her staff were caught in heavy gunfire, and they suffered repeated shelling from enemy artillery. Each time this happened they had to abandon their hospitals and suspend the vital, life-saving work until they could open new ones further from the front line. Then, in March 1917, the Russian ruler, Tsar Nicholas II, was suddenly overthrown in a violent revolution. He was later brutally murdered, along with his wife and children, and their bodies thrown down a mine. By November a bloody civil war was being fought across Russia as rival groups struggled to seize power for themselves.

The danger to Inglis and her volunteers got worse as the civil war developed into the deadliest the world had ever seen. It eventually cost more than nine million lives, most of them ordinary civilians, but Inglis refused to go back to Scotland. She was too tired and too ill to operate on patients, but she said she wouldn't leave Russia until she could be sure that the exhausted Serbian troops would also be safe.

The British Royal Navy finally agreed to help them escape, but only after weeks of arguing. Their warships were needed because the appalling savagery of the civil war had made it impossible for anyone to travel through Russia safely, even armed soldiers. The continuing world war similarly meant that the most convenient route home (through countries such as France and Belgium) was also out of the question. As a result, the only way that Inglis, her volunteers and the Serbians could escape was by making a lengthy sea voyage across the Arctic Ocean.

The voyage home from the remote port of Archangel was rough and uncomfortable. Inglis grew weaker and weaker as the ship neared northern England. When she collapsed, it must have been clear to everyone that she was dying, but she still struggled into her uniform as the ship docked at Newcastle. Inglis was determined to salute her courageous volunteers one last time, but she died the following morning.

Elsie's important work continued without her, and her staff carried on treating the sick and injured until the very end of World War I. They had saved several hundred thousand lives by the time the hospitals were handed over to the civilian authorities – and nearly five years had passed since their inspired and energetic creator had been told to 'go home and sit still'.

Harry Jones and Cedric Hill

A Magical Double Act (Turkey, 1918)

Cedric Hill was an Australian airman who served in Britain's Royal Flying Corps during World War I. In May 1916 he was flying low over Egypt's vast Sinai Desert when his aircraft was shot down by Turkish troops. He wasn't injured and spent six hours trying to defend himself with a machine gun, before having to surrender after running out of ammunition. Hill was taken prisoner by soldiers in the Ottoman army, which was fighting on the side of Austria and Germany against Britain and France.

Shortly afterwards, he was fortunate enough to meet a British army officer who had been captured following a long siege at Kut-el-Amara in what is now Iraq. Harry Jones had been forced to march more than 2,000 kilometres across Asia Minor to a prison-of-war camp at Yozgad in modern-day Turkey. Once he arrived he quickly became friends with his fellow prisoner, Cedric Hill.

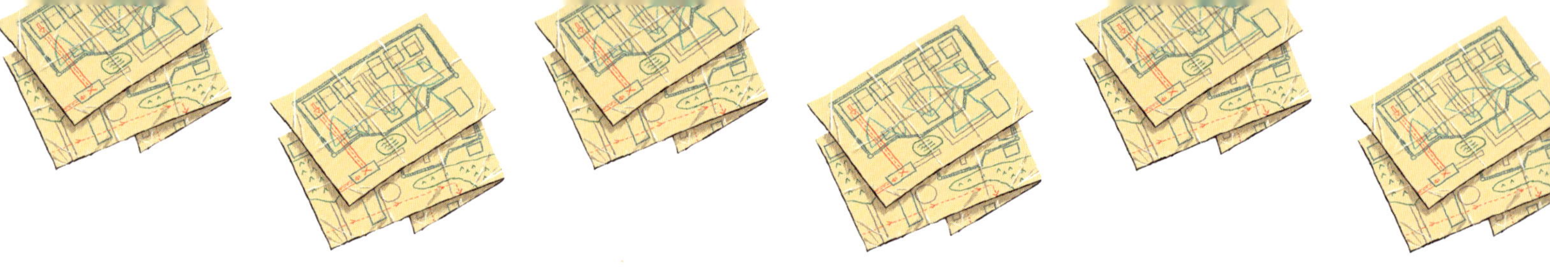

Yozgad was notorious. Prisoners were never given enough food to eat, and the guards boasted that its remote location, surrounded by mountains and desert, meant that it was virtually impossible for anyone to escape. However, spending time as a POW was often very boring, and the inmates had a lot of spare time in which to think up cunning escape plans.

Hill had been an amateur magician before the war, and to help their fellow prisoners cope with the boredom the two friends began entertaining them with magic tricks and a home-made Ouija board. This is a device that some people believe can be used to talk to ghosts and the spirits of friends and relatives who have died. Hill and Jones didn't believe this for a minute, but they enjoyed playing with the board and it amused their audiences.

The two men had a lot of fun putting on their shows, but they still felt it was their duty as military officers to escape from Yozgad. However, one of the difficulties they faced was that the prison guards had threatened to punish or even kill some of the prisoners if anyone else in the camp managed to escape. Hill and Jones couldn't let this happen, so they had to think of a way to get out without it looking like they had escaped. They thought one possibility might be to involve the guards in such a way that they would never be able to tell anyone else what had happened. If the guards helped them to escape and couldn't admit what they had done, then they might not feel the need to punish or kill any of the prisoners who were left behind.

Every POW knew that attempting to escape was dangerous, but after more than a year in captivity Hill and Jones were still keen to do it and thought that their Ouija board might

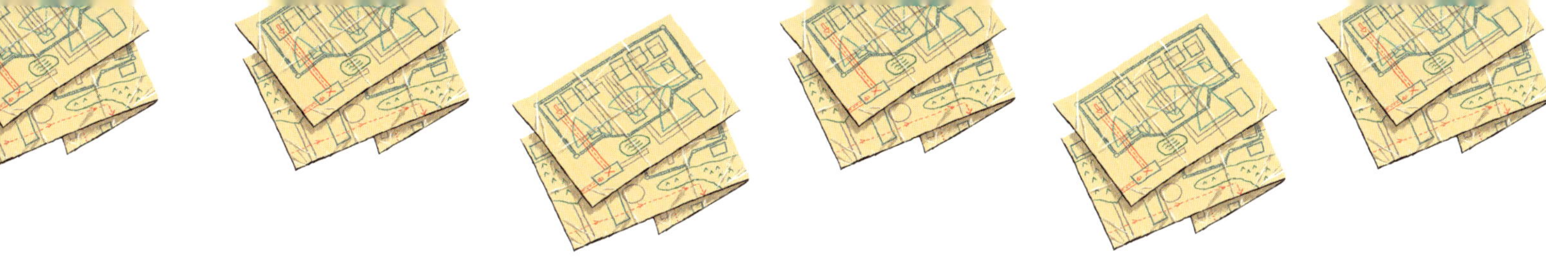

help them get away with it. Both of them had noticed that the camp commandant was very interested in what they were doing with the board. His name was Kiazim, and he was in charge of all the guards at Yozgad. They watched him very closely for several weeks and began to suspect that he thought all their magic was genuine and their made-up ghosts really existed.

Kiazim also had a reputation around the camp for being very greedy. He was always talking about money and expensive things, and he became wildly excited when Jones mentioned to him one day that they had been talking to a ghost who claimed to know the whereabouts of some buried gold. The greedy commandant immediately decided that he had to have this treasure for himself. He kept asking Hill and Jones to speak to the ghost again to find out where it was. Because he wanted the treasure so badly, he didn't suspect the whole thing was a trick, even when the two men began calling the ghost they had invented 'the Spook'.

Once it became clear that Kiazim believed the Spook to be real, Jones told him that the ghost would only reveal where the treasure was buried once the two friends had been released from the prison camp and allowed to travel to the coast. Both of them thought that it would be easier to escape from Turkey if they could reach the sea, but they must have wondered whether even greedy Kiazim would fall for such an outrageous lie. But, amazingly, he did. Greed sometimes makes people do extraordinary things, and after several months Kiazim

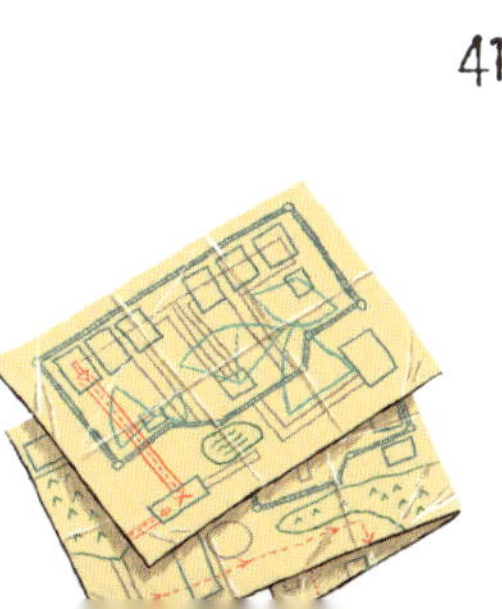

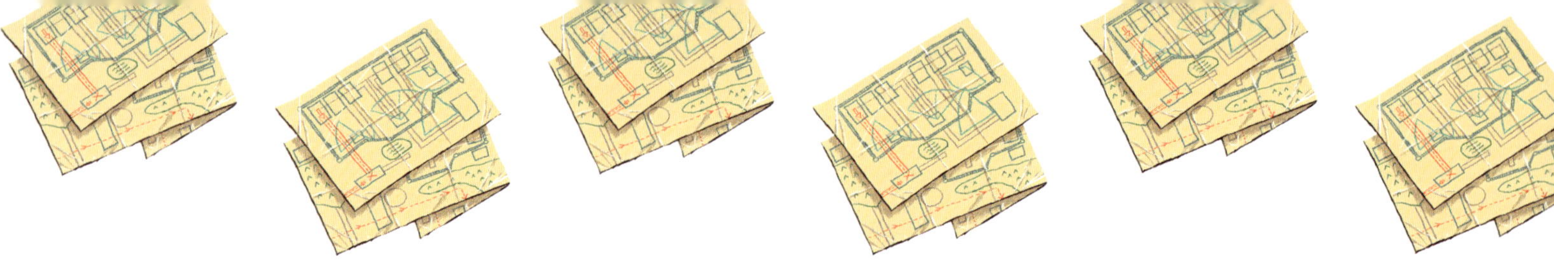

had become so desperate to get his hands on the gold that he agreed to help the two men escape from his own prison camp.

However, even an important commandant can't just decide to release a couple of prisoners. Luckily, Jones had already thought of this and suggested to Kiazim that he and Hill should pretend to be ill. The commandant loved this idea. He saw it as a way to get them out of the camp and get himself closer to the Spook's buried treasure.

Jones thought it would be easier to fake the symptoms of a mental illness rather than a physical one, and Hill agreed to give it a try. Both of them started behaving very oddly, continuing like this for several months, until Kiazim decided it was safe to arrange for them to be transferred to a nearby hospital where their 'illness' could be treated properly.

Kiazim had been relatively easy to trick because his greedy nature meant he really wanted to believe everything the men told him. But Hill and Jones guessed that convincing actual doctors would be much harder, so they faked a suicide attempt to make it look as though they really were very ill. Obviously, they only wanted to make it look as though they were trying to kill themselves, but the attempt went so badly wrong that they almost succeeded! Fortunately, the lives of both men were saved by quick-thinking staff at the hospital. The experience was terrifying, but in a strange way it worked because all the staff now believed that Hill and Jones were seriously ill, and one of the doctors arranged for them to be sent to a better hospital several hundred kilometres away in Constantinople, the Ottoman capital on the coast.

The friends' original plan had been to reach the sea and then find a way to board a ship. Both thought they could reach Cyprus this way, an island that was still in British hands. Unfortunately, staff at the hospital in Constantinople were now so worried about the two men's condition that they were constantly watched to make sure they didn't try to kill themselves again.

According to Jones, this experience was almost as bad as Yozgad had been. The two men couldn't talk to each other, and spending weeks and weeks pretending to be ill was so stressful that it really did begin to affect their mental health. By October 1918 both of them were exhausted and confused and in such terrible shape mentally that the Turks finally agreed to ship them back to England on compassionate grounds. This meant their escape plan had finally worked, even if the whole thing had taken so long that the Ottoman army had actually surrendered by the time the two men got home. World War I itself ended barely a week later, but their achievement was still very real. Jones and Hill had successfully tricked their way out of Yozgad, harming no one in the process – except, for a while, themselves.

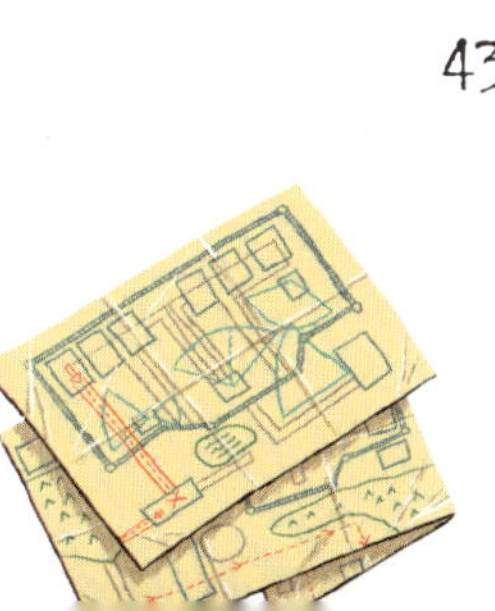

The Holzminden Ten

Digging for Victory (Germany, 1918)

Holzminden was a huge prison camp in Germany during World War I, and one of the very worst. The main building was a disused army barracks that had been hastily converted to accommodate about six hundred prisoners. Most were British soldiers, sailors and airmen, but the barracks were cold, crowded and very uncomfortable. The men often had to cook their meals outside, even in the middle of winter, and sometimes food was so scarce that they had only one meal a day.

The commandant was a vicious bully called Karl Niemeyer, whose twin brother was in charge of another POW camp about 80 kilometres away. Niemeyer seemed to hate every single inmate at Holzminden and enjoyed torturing them whenever he could think of a reason to do so. One prisoner was locked in an underground cell for three days just for smiling, while others were severely punished for wearing shorts.

His most famous victim was a twenty-one-year-old pilot who had shot down a German airship in 1916. William Leefe Robinson had been awarded a rare Victoria Cross for this, Britain's highest military medal, but he crashed his aircraft a few months later and was taken prisoner. He was sent to Holzminden, where he was so badly abused by Niemeyer that he never really recovered.

Many prisoners, including Robinson, tried several times to escape from the camp. Some attempted to cut through the barbed wire which surrounded the prison. Others tried walking out through the main gate dressed as German guards. One inmate even disguised himself as a woman. The record number of attempts by an individual in the camp was at least eight, but by July 1918 no one had been successful. Even the few who did manage to get out of the camp were captured and brought back long before they had reached the safety of the Dutch border nearly 250 kilometres away.

By the summer of 1918 the war was almost over, but none of the inmates could have known this, which is why so many were still trying hard to escape from the brutal Niemeyer and his guards. One large and very well-organised group of officers had spent nearly nine months excavating a tunnel. Eventually, this stretched for more than 50 metres under the barbed-wire fence and towards a neighbouring farmer's field. Even with the right tools this would have been enormously difficult, but because prisoners weren't allowed any, the men had to make do with whatever they could find around the camp. This included kitchen spoons and bowls, which were used to scratch through the hard, packed mud and scoop it up.

The lack of tools is the main reason why the tunnel was so narrow and why it took so long to dig. (When it was finished it was only just large enough for a person to crawl through.) Another reason is that only two or three diggers could work in the tunnel at a time, and they could dig for just a few hours each day. If they stayed below ground for any longer, the guards would have become suspicious and started wondering where the inmates had gone.

With dozens of these armed guards in and around the camp, everything had to be done as quietly as possible. There were also numerous technical difficulties that had to be overcome: for example, all the soil the men scooped out had to be stored somewhere Niemeyer's guards wouldn't find it, while everyone working underground needed a supply of fresh air to stop them from suffocating.

The air problem was cleverly solved by rigging up a sort of 'chimney' made from empty food tins. This fed air into the tunnel while the soil the men removed was put into sacks and dragged back to the entrance. Pieces of wood taken from the men's own bed frames were used as supports to prevent the tunnel roof from collapsing on to the diggers.

The inmates had made the sacks by cutting and stitching their old clothes together. Once filled with earth, they were stored in a small disused room beneath the barracks.

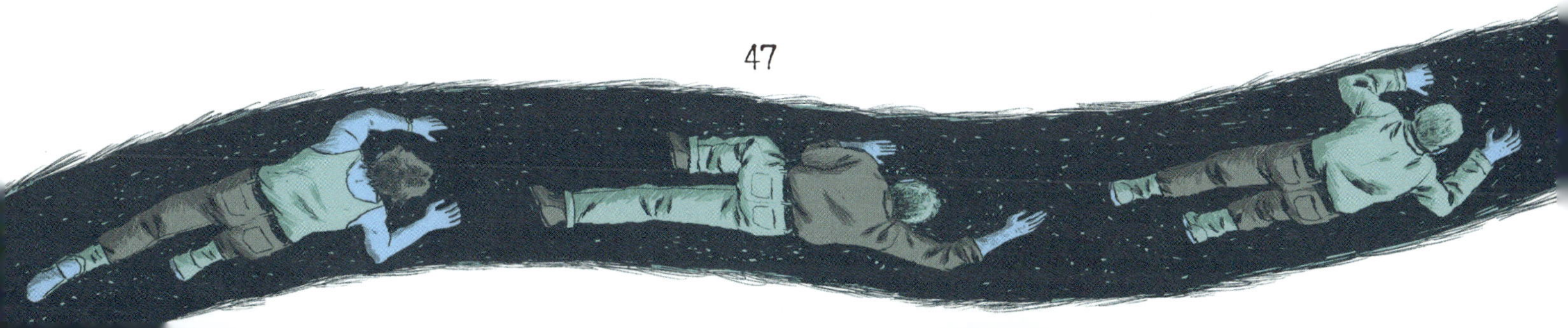

However, because Niemeyer had issued an order forbidding British officers to enter this part of the building, the group had to construct a secret hatch so they could reach it from the outside. Once this was done the sacks could be smuggled into the storeroom and stashed out of sight.

While a small team took turns digging and filling the sacks, other inmates were busy making false identity papers and modifying their military uniforms to look more like civilian clothing. Altogether more than eighty prisoners were involved in these activities, making this the largest escape attempt of the entire war.

For a while the diggers were worried that they had not tunnelled quite far enough to come up in the farmer's field, but by July they were confident they had and work stopped at last. The night of the 23rd was selected as the most suitable date to make a run for it, and everyone agreed that the men who had done the most digging deserved to be the first to crawl through the tunnel.

Everyone was very nervous, but for the first few minutes everything went according to plan. In fact, the tunnel stopped just short of the field, but some tall bean plants close to the barbed-wire fence made it possible for the escapees to reach the field without being seen by the guards. The first twenty-nine prisoners crawled through one at a time, before climbing out at the other end and running into the field, but then disaster struck.

The diggers hadn't fitted enough supports in the tunnel because they couldn't steal more wood without the guards noticing what they had done. As the thirtieth escapee made his way into the tunnel, a couple of props suddenly shifted and broke and the tunnel caved in on top of him. Fortunately, Jack Straw wasn't harmed by the collapse, but the tunnel was completely blocked and now no one else could use it.

This was bitterly disappointing after so many months' work, especially as nineteen of the men who had got out of the camp were immediately recaptured when the farmer reported them for trampling all over his crops. All were sent back to face an angry Commandant Niemeyer, which meant that just ten men were left to find their way safely out of Germany. Remarkably, all of them made it, although they had to split up to avoid detection. One managed to reach the Netherlands in just three days because he spoke excellent German and had found a train which took him all the way to the border. But it was much harder for the others, who had to make the same long journey entirely on foot. This meant travelling without maps, usually after dark to avoid enemy patrols, and hiding in woods and ditches whenever they needed to rest.

With no money these men had very little to eat, and they took an average of two weeks to reach the UK. After getting home one of them sent a delighted message back to Germany on behalf of the whole group. It was addressed to Commandant Niemeyer and read: 'HAVING A LOVELY TIME. IF I EVER FIND YOU IN LONDON I WILL BREAK YOUR NECK.'

Yoshie Shiratori

A Little Fisherman Flees Four Times (Japan, 1936)

Yoshie Shiratori worked as a crab fisherman but never had much money because he loved gambling and wasn't very good at it. He often lost more than he earned, so he started stealing from other people to pay his bills. In 1936 he was involved in a fight over money. The other person died, and Shiratori was arrested and charged with robbery and murder.

Shiratori always claimed he was innocent, saying it was an accident, but it's impossible to know if this is true or not. What happened next made him a strange sort of hero in Japan, and there have been so many stories told about him that it's hard to know which are real and which are made up.

While waiting to be tried in court, Shiratori was sent to his local prison in Aomori. According to the stories, he immediately began looking for a way to escape. Like many thieves, he already knew how to unlock a door without a key and didn't think the prison locks looked more difficult than any others. All he needed was a metal strip bent into the right shape to fit

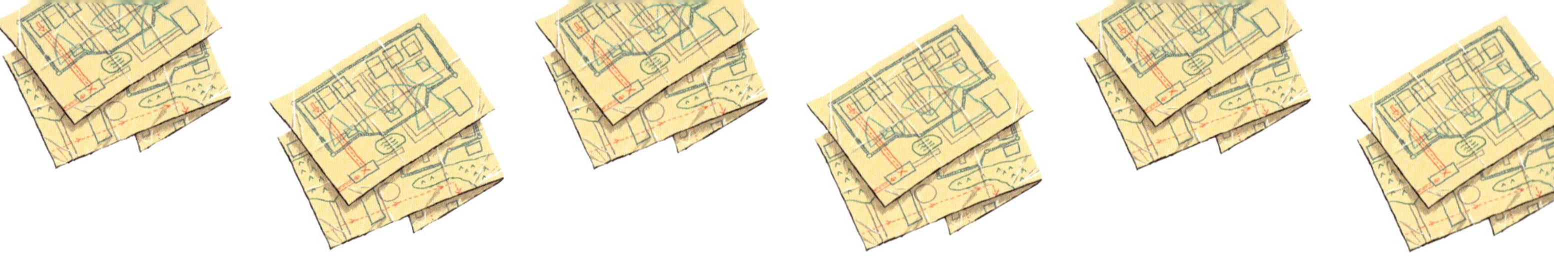

the lock, and he soon found the perfect piece attached to the wooden bucket prisoners used for washing in their cells.

The guards were more of a problem, although Shiratori knew they couldn't keep an eye on him the whole time. He began observing a number of them, and after a few weeks he noticed that each guard had a fixed routine and stuck to exactly the same timetable when patrolling the cells and the prison grounds. It took him several more weeks to work out the routines of all the guards in his part of the prison. From this he calculated that if he timed things correctly, he would have nearly fifteen minutes between patrols to break out of his cell and escape from the prison without anyone seeing him.

His plan was relatively simple, and it worked perfectly. Shiratori used the piece of metal to unlock five or six different doors and found himself in a corridor leading out to the street. Seconds later he was free and had successfully completed the first of his four escapes.

Unfortunately, the police caught him just three days later, when he tried to rob a hospital because he needed food and money. This time he was taken to court and given a life sentence for robbery and murder. He was then transferred to a different prison, in Akita, which the court believed to be more secure than the one in Aomori.

The new prison had special cells for prisoners who had already managed to escape from somewhere else. The only window in Shiratori's cell was a small skylight set into the centre of

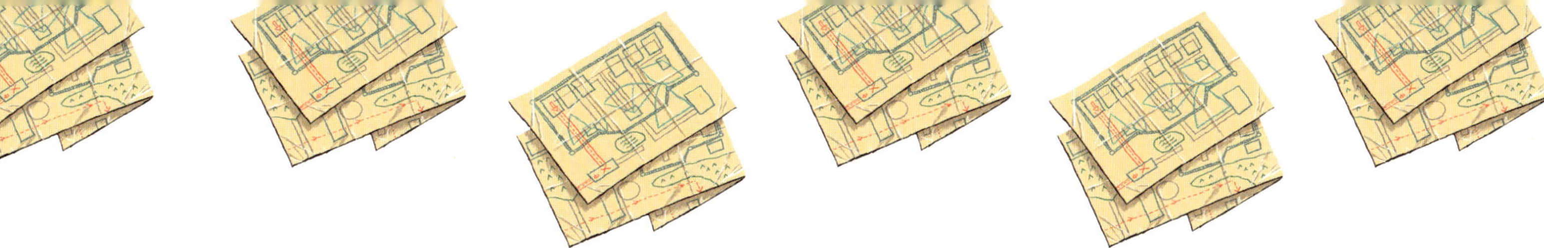

the high ceiling. Even if he could pick the lock of the cell door again, there were many more guards than there had been in Aomori. Their routines were much harder to understand than before, but although one of them seemed quite friendly, it seemed the skylight was Shiratori's only way out. It had several steel bars across it to stop anyone climbing through, but they were set into an old wooden frame. Shiratori thought he could probably loosen the frame or even break it if he spent long enough trying. To do this he had to claw his way up the cell wall each night, moving as quietly as possible and being careful to do so only when there were no guards outside his cell door. In this way he managed to loosen the frame bit by bit and after several weeks was able to remove a couple of the bars.

Climbing through the skylight would enable Shiratori to get on to the roof of the prison, but he waited for a stormy night so the prison guards wouldn't hear him walking around on the tiles. Once he got to the roof he was able to jump over the prison wall, and he was free again.

This time Shiratori managed to remain on the loose for several months, but then he made the mistake of visiting the friendly prison guard. He tried to explain that he hadn't killed the man during the fight and that the whole thing had been an accident. The guard pretended to believe this, but then called the police as soon as Shiratori went to the bathroom. They arrived a few minutes later to arrest him and took him back to Akita under heavy guard.

Several years passed before Shiratori was moved from Akita. This time he was taken to a prison called Abashiri, in the north of Japan. This was a very tough jail where many of Japan's worst, most violent prisoners were kept locked up in very harsh conditions. Shiratori later said he was made to wear summer clothes even in the frozen depths of winter, and that he was frequently beaten up by the guards. All his meals were passed to him through a narrow slot in the cell door and he was handcuffed to stop him attempting another escape. Apparently, the metal handcuffs were unlocked only when it was time for his weekly wash.

Shiratori found these conditions unbearable and was determined to escape for a third time. Most days the prisoners were given miso soup to eat, and he started dripping it on to the handcuffs and the frame around the slot in the door. Gradually, over months and months, this rusted the metal and weakened it. Eventually, it was possible for Shiratori to pull the handcuffs off and remove part of the frame surrounding the rectangular slot in the door. This made the opening slightly larger, but it was still very small. Shiratori wasn't a big man, however, and he wondered if it would be possible to squeeze through the slot by dislocating his shoulders. Dislocation means using extreme force to separate the bones that make up the joints in our bodies. It is very painful and extremely dangerous because bones can be broken or permanently damaged when this happens. Most dislocations happen by accident, but Shiratori was desperate and couldn't think of a better way to escape from Abashiri and its cruel guards.

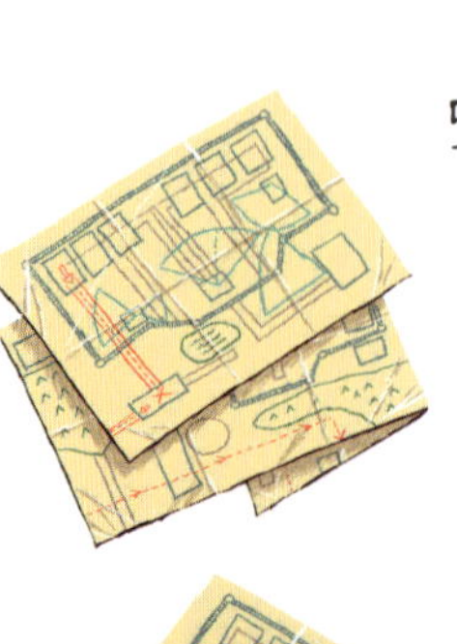

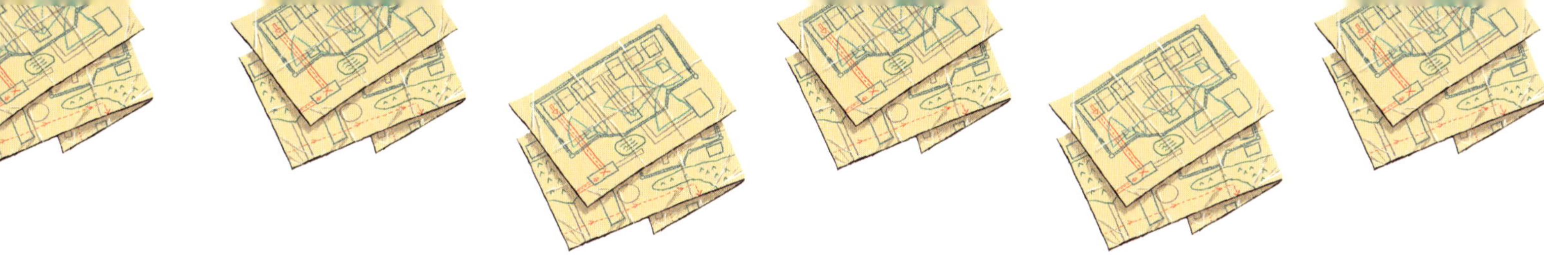

By August 1944 he had finally plucked up the courage to put his painful plan into action. One night he forced one or both of his shoulders to dislocate, and this was enough for him to wriggle through the slot and disappear into the darkness. Fleeing as fast as he could on foot, he hid first in an abandoned mine and then later in the high mountains that surround Abashiri. Shiratori seems to have survived for a long time by killing small animals and eating wild berries, but after two years he was caught stealing food from a remote farm. Another fight broke out, and the farmer was fatally stabbed. Shiratori was arrested but insisted he was acting in self-defence. Many didn't believe his story, and several newspapers started running stories with headlines about 'the man no prison can hold'.

The authorities didn't believe he was innocent either, and Shiratori was sentenced to death by a judge and sent to Sapporo prison to await his execution. There he was put into a cell with a skylight so small that even his head wouldn't fit through it and with a strong steel door that miso soup couldn't weaken. Luckily for Shiratori, the guards were so confident he couldn't escape from the cell that they didn't bother putting him in handcuffs. Also, because everyone was so sure that the skylight and door were escape-proof, no one thought about the floor. It didn't take Shiratori long to think about it, however. Very soon he had lifted a couple of floorboards and begun digging his way out of Sapporo using one of the metal bowls prisoners were given for their meals.

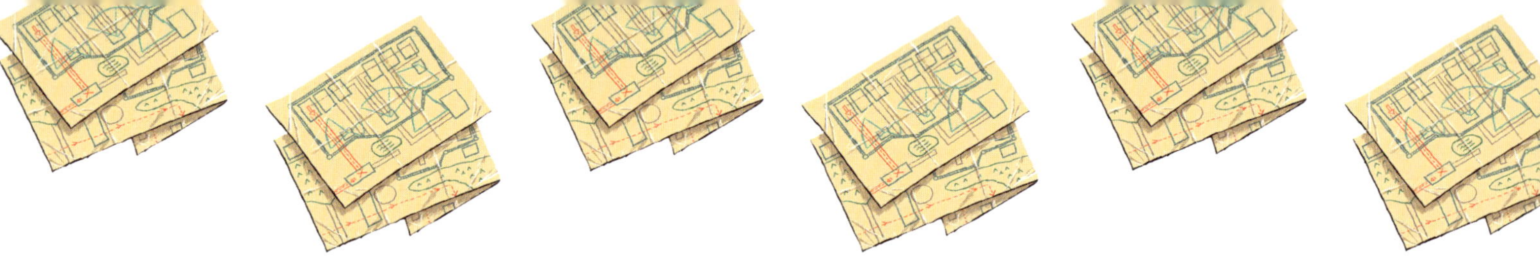

But this time the story has a very different ending. Shiratori escaped, as usual, but then surrendered and gave himself up to the police. In court he successfully argued that he hadn't meant to kill the farmer, that the second fight he was in really was self-defence, and this time a judge decided he was telling the truth.

Shiratori wasn't set free, though, because the judge said he still had to be punished for all his other crimes. However, he was clearly impressed that the prisoner hadn't attacked any guards while escaping, even though so many of them had treated him very badly over the years. For this reason, the judge agreed to send Shiratori to a prison in Tokyo where the conditions were fairer than before. He was also released much earlier than expected, partly because of his good behaviour, but also because for the first time in his life Yoshie Shiratori hadn't tried to escape.

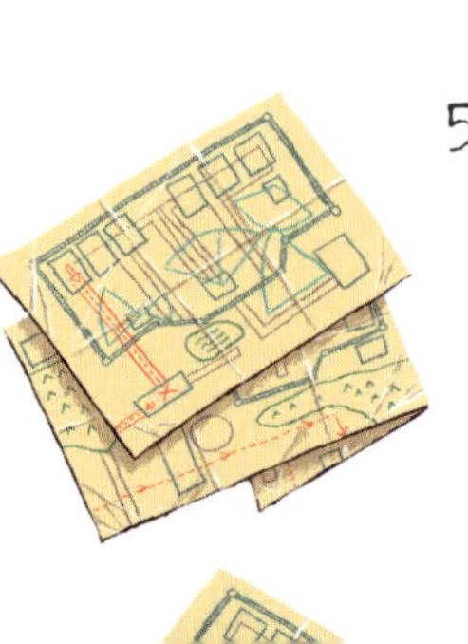

Chaim Herszman

A Teen with a Gift for Disguise (Poland, 1940)

More than a million innocent men, women and children were imprisoned in ghettos when the German army invaded much of Europe during World War II. These ghettos were areas of towns and cities where particular groups of people were forced to live in filthy, overcrowded conditions. They were cut off from normal everyday life and separated by walls and high wire fences from other residents.

Most of the people in these ghettos were Jews, although other minorities were also persecuted by the Germans in this way, albeit in smaller numbers: for example, Europe's largest ghetto, in the Polish capital Warsaw, contained nearly half a million Jews and several hundred Roma, Sinti and other minorities. Armed guards surrounded each ghetto, and no one was allowed to enter or leave without a special permit. Food was always very scarce and the living conditions so crowded and unhygienic that many either starved to death or died of horrible diseases such as typhus and diphtheria.

Even if an individual managed to survive this experience, the ghetto was for most just the starting point of a terrible journey that ended when entire families were murdered in what were known as 'concentration camps'. The largest was Auschwitz, where more than a million people were deliberately tortured and killed over a five-year period. The camps were an important part of German leader Adolf Hitler's plan to murder millions of innocent civilians, including all of Europe's Jews.

Poland's second-largest ghetto was in Łódź. Beginning in February 1940, more than 200,000 Jews were ordered to move into a tiny area of the city that was surrounded by barbed wire. Their only 'crime' was being Jewish, and thousands of them were forced to work long hours under conditions of slavery making German military uniforms. Even very young children had to do this, while living in old tumbledown buildings without heating, running water or proper sewers.

This combination of hard labour, disease and starvation killed nearly a quarter of the ghetto's population, but escape was almost impossible. Besides the barbed wire, guards and guns, non-Jews living nearby were told they would be severely punished if they helped anyone run away. Sharing food, medicine or even clothing with a Jew was also a serious crime. Yet despite these extraordinary challenges, a few inmates somehow managed to escape, and one of the first was a remarkable thirteen-year-old Polish boy called Chaim Herszman.

Herszman knew he had to get out of the ghetto because he had stabbed a guard who'd threatened to shoot his younger brother, Srulek. The two boys had been trying to steal some food for their parents, when eleven-year-old Srulek got caught on a barbed-wire fence. As the guard raised his weapon to shoot, Herszman ran at him and plunged a small knife into his stomach. The guard bled to death, and Herszman knew that he would be killed as soon as the Germans found out what he had done.

Herszman was a clever boy and spoke several different languages, including German. He also had blond hair and blue eyes, which meant that people often didn't realise he was Jewish. These were useful things for a child whose long journey to freedom would involve travelling thousands of kilometres through enemy territory.

First he tried to flee to Russia, which his older brother had done days before Łódź's Jews were ordered into the ghetto. Sneaking out of the ghetto, Herszman joined a small group of refugees, telling them he was Catholic and that his name was Henryk Karbowski. He hoped they would help him find a way across the frozen River Bug, but the group was suddenly ambushed by Russian soldiers throwing explosive grenades. Most of the refugees were killed immediately, but Herszman escaped and decided to head for France, which Germany hadn't yet invaded.

He managed to sneak on to a train and found a hiding place in one of the carriages. To his horror, he then realised it was a troop train, meaning that it was full of soldiers returning to

Germany. When his hiding place was discovered, he explained he was a German boy living in Poland and that his parents had been murdered a few weeks earlier by some Russians. Herszman was such a good liar that the soldiers believed his story. One of them felt so sorry for him that when the train reached Berlin, he took the boy home with him to meet his wife and daughter.

It turned out the soldier and his wife were both Catholics, like Herszman claimed to be. They agreed to help by giving him a set of German clothes and some false identity papers in the name of Karl-Heinz Reitzenstein. This meant the thirteen-year-old now not only looked German and spoke the language, but had documents showing that he was indeed German.

Herszman stayed with the family for several weeks but knew that Germany's capital was an incredibly dangerous place for him to be. In June 1940 he spotted an opportunity to get away when the French army surrendered to Germany. This made France much less safe for a Jew than it had been, but it gave Herszman a brilliant idea.

Polish prisoners were being sent to France to work as slave labourers. As Herszman could speak both Polish and German, he thought he would be able to find work as a translator. The soldier and his wife agreed and arranged for him to go to a farm in France. He was soon busy translating the German farm manager's orders so that the new Polish workers could understand them. Later on, still pretending to be German, he found a job in a company nearby that made agricultural equipment.

Successful escapes usually involve luck as well as courage and determination. At least once, Herszman came dangerously close to being found out after falling ill and ending up in hospital. With a high temperature and feeling confused, he was overheard mumbling something to himself in Yiddish. This is a language spoken by many Polish Jews, and on hearing it a member of the medical staff realised that Herszman was probably not really German. Incredibly, the teenager managed to slip away before he was arrested and, after stealing a farm vehicle, drove several hundred kilometres south, where he thought he would be safer.

Unfortunately, he wasn't at all safe. Not long after arriving in the south, Herszman was stopped and questioned by the police. This time his lies weren't believed, and he was taken to a police station and put in a room to await further interrogation. Once again, luck came to the rescue. Not only was the door to the room left unlocked, but when Herszman crept out of the building he found an unlocked police car parked outside. He hid in the back and a few hours later was driven out of German-occupied France – by a policeman!

Over the next few months Herszman changed his name and identity several more times. He waited until he could cross the mountains from France into Spain, and eventually made his way to the British port of Gibraltar. Polish refugees were welcome there and, like many of them, Herszman decided to join the British armed forces to continue the fight against Germany and Japan.

Herszman now changed his name for one last time, to the more English-sounding Henry Carr, and survived the war, although several members of his family did not, including his brother Srulek. Afterwards he moved to England and got married, and for a long time no one knew his real name or his story, not even his wife and children. In the end it took more than ten years before he felt safe enough to reveal his true identity, to admit he was a Polish Jew, and to talk about his remarkable escape from the Łódź ghetto.

Lillian Gutteridge

Dunkirk's Last Angel (France, 1940)

After almost a year of fighting, Britain and its allies faced the real possibility that they could be defeated by Germany and lose World War II. At the end of May 1940 more than 330,000 mostly British and French soldiers had been beaten back to the coast of northern France. All of them were then forced to flee across the English Channel to avoid being caught by the seemingly unstoppable German army as it swept through Holland and Belgium on its way to capture Paris.

The emergency evacuation of these troops was centred on the small French town of Dunkirk. Hundreds of vessels were hastily sent from England to bring them back, everything from Royal Navy warships to private yachts and even small rowing boats manned by incredibly courageous volunteers.

The fleet crossing the Channel was one of the largest ever assembled, but the losses over the next few days were enormous. Although not a single British soldier was left behind on

the beaches, nearly 62,000 men and women were killed, wounded or taken prisoner. More than two hundred vessels were lost at sea, and eighty-four British aircraft shot down. An astonishing 76,000 tons of ammunition had to be abandoned, along with 400,000 tons of military supplies and around 2,500 big guns and other pieces of artillery.

The rapid rescue of so many battle-weary troops is now regarded as one of the great triumphs of the war, but it very nearly ended in disaster. The fact that it didn't was the result of countless examples of personal heroism, including that of Lillian Gutteridge. Despite being badly wounded herself, she courageously defended several injured soldiers and helped them and many others to escape back to England.

Hundreds of women volunteers of all ages had been posted to France by this time, although in the 1940s they were not allowed to fight alongside the men. Many worked instead as army drivers, medics, radio operators and even spies, but Gutteridge was a highly respected member of the Queen Alexandra's Imperial Military Nursing Service, or QAs. Like the women who serve in the modern-day Queen Alexandra's Royal Army Nursing Corps, her job was difficult and dangerous, and frequently brought her into close contact with the enemy.

Courageous QAs saw action in many different countries between 1939 and 1945, including ones in Africa and Asia, as well as in Europe. In Dunkirk, they played a vital role in the miraculous mass evacuation of soldiers and terrified civilians from France. The people they saved called them the 'Angels of Dunkirk', and Gutteridge is now believed to have been the very last angel to get out of France.

In early June Gutteridge was racing towards the French coast in an old ambulance when she was spotted by a German officer. The vehicle was full of soldiers on stretchers, and they had already had an exceptionally difficult and frightening journey. The roads in this part of France were blocked by fleeing soldiers and the smoking remains of burned-out vehicles that had been bombed and strafed (or machine-gunned) by enemy pilots. Gutteridge could see from the officer's uniform that he was a member of the SS, the German security police, which had a reputation for terrible brutality and even mass murder. She was afraid that if she didn't drive on, she wouldn't get to the coast in time for her patients to board a vessel and escape. However, the officer was armed, so she had no alternative but to pull over and stop.

The officer ordered her at gunpoint to switch off the engine and surrender both the ambulance and her patients to his hated organisation. Gutteridge feared for the lives of the wounded men and so refused to hand them over. This led to an angry argument, during which she slapped the officer in the face. He was surprised by her fury and quickly responded by stabbing her with his dagger. She was lucky he didn't just shoot her, and very fortunate that a Scottish soldier who was passing by pulled out his own gun and shot the German dead before things got any worse.

The dagger had nevertheless caused a vicious wound to her thigh. Gutteridge was bleeding badly but was determined to press on despite being in great pain. Hauling herself back into the ambulance, she drove as fast as she could to a nearby railway depot. Here she found a French train driver who was heading to another Channel port called Cherbourg. In a few minutes she had managed to persuade him to carry her wounded patients the rest of the way to the coast.

As the train chugged north, she repeatedly asked the driver to stop at various places along the way so that other stranded soldiers could come on board. He eventually agreed to this and more than six hundred wounded men were transported to the coast in this way. Fortunately, some vessels that could carry them to safety were still waiting at Cherbourg harbour, including one staffed by army medics and QAs. Its captain later described how Gutteridge's nursing colleagues worked calmly and efficiently, treating the most severely injured as bombs fell close by and the sound of gunfire continued all around.

Happily, and despite remaining in France until the last possible hour, all of the QAs made it back across the English Channel. Lillian Gutteridge was among the very last to escape, but she was treated for her injuries when she reached England and went on to make a full recovery.

Witold Gliński

The Longest Walk (Russia, 1941)

More than ten years after World War II ended a former Polish army officer called Sławomir Rawicz published a book about his miraculous escape from a Siberian prison camp in 1941. In *The Long Walk* he described how he broke out of the camp during a blizzard and then spent nearly a year trekking thousands of kilometres through Russia, Mongolia and China to reach a British army base in India. The book sold more than half a million copies, was translated into dozens of different languages, and was then made into an Oscar-nominated film. The only trouble was, *The Long Walk* was just one possible version of the story.

Years after its publication a television documentary revealed that although many of the events described in the book were probably true, they had nothing to do with Rawicz. The programme proved that he couldn't have been the Polish soldier who managed to escape from Siberia in the middle of winter, although he had spent some time in a Russian prison. Nor could he have been the man who risked his life crossing the Himalayas and the scorching Gobi Desert before rejoining the Polish army to defeat the Nazis.

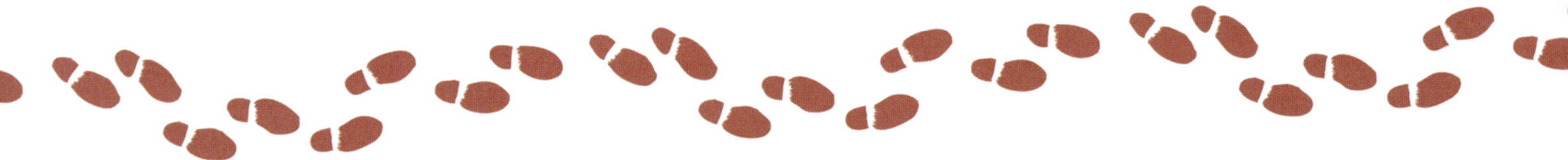

When the truth came out about Rawicz, another Polish soldier admitted to a journalist that actually he was the book's real hero. Witold Gliński had never met Rawicz, either before or after *The Long Walk* went on sale, and now both men have died it's impossible to be sure how one of them managed to steal the other's story. All we know is that Gliński said nothing about his escape for well over half a century (even his wife didn't know about it), but that when his version emerged, it was, if anything, even more astonishing than Rawicz's tale.

Gliński told the journalist that he was only a teenager when he was put to work outside the prison camp as a lumberjack, and this gave him the perfect opportunity to look for an escape route. He realised he couldn't get back to Poland, which had been invaded by the German army, so he decided to head eastwards instead. The idea to do this had come to him after he had studied an old map of Asia hanging above a radio that the prison commandant's wife had asked him to mend.

Maria Uszakof must have taken pity on the teenager, knowing that he and the other prisoners had to share simple wooden huts in a part of the world where temperatures plunge well below freezing every winter. She gave him a piece of dried meat and some warm clothes, exactly the sort of supplies that a young man would need if he was setting off on a long journey at that time of year.

Gliński was aware that February was probably the very worst time to attempt an escape, except for one important thing: with the temperature dropping as low as –25°C, he felt sure

the Russian guards would be sheltering inside instead of patrolling the area around the camp, looking for possible escapees.

His plan was to wait until midnight and then scramble under the wire fence as quickly as he could. That way he would have several hours of darkness in which to get as far away from the camp as possible without anyone seeing him. When he tried this a couple of nights later, he was spotted by several other prisoners as he left his hut. Watching him digging under the wire fence, they decided to follow him, expecting the youngster to lead them all to safety.

Gliński explained that his plan wasn't very well thought out. They would have to walk at least twenty hours a day, he whispered, and if that sounded too hard, they should go back under the wire or wait to be recaptured. The border was at least 2,500 kilometres away, but nevertheless three other Polish soldiers decided to go with him, together with an American, a Yugoslavian and a Ukrainian.

None of the seven had been friends in the camp, Gliński said later. They were just ordinary people who had to rely on each other and work together in order to survive. There was very little conversation between them because of this, but Gliński emerged as their natural leader as they slowly tramped through the bitterly cold forest landscape.

Gliński had grown up in the countryside, so he already knew which berries and fungi were safe to eat and which were deadly. He also knew where to catch fish and how to cook

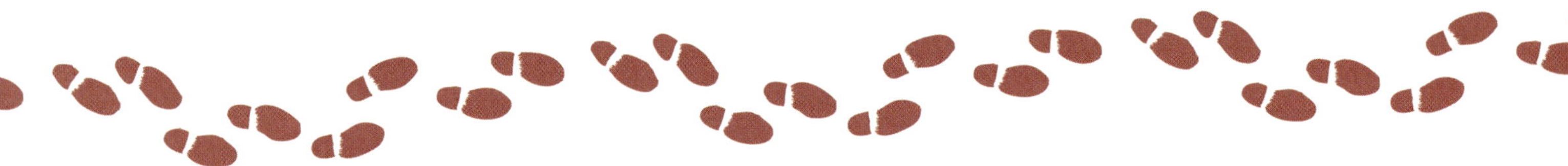

them, and when one of the group stumbled upon a wounded deer trapped in a ravine, it was Gliński who showed everyone how to kill and skin it. The deer's skin was used to repair their boots, while the meat provided something of a feast. It lasted for several days, even though there were seven of them, but eating this well was an exceptionally rare treat. Most of the time Gliński and the others were dangerously close to starvation. Nature was now their real enemy, not Russians with guns. Prowling wolves and even bears had to be chased off, and the men endured a seemingly endless struggle to keep going through some of the most hostile environments on the planet.

Things got no easier when they left the frozen wastes of the Siberian forest behind and entered the Gobi Desert. The largest desert in Asia, it straddles Mongolia and China, and covers almost 1.3 million square kilometres. That's approximately ten times the size of England, but almost no one lives there. Cold winds whipping across the landscape mean the temperature in winter often falls to –40°C, but in summer the air gets so thick and hot that travellers find it hard to breathe.

The Gobi is also one of the driest places on Earth, so not much thrives there except thorny plants and grass, poisonous snakes and a rare species of camel that survives by eating snow. By the time Gliński and the others reached here, however, the snows were long gone and had been replaced by a burning sun. It was usually easier to travel after dark because of this, but here too, unsurprisingly, the men often couldn't find enough to eat or drink. At times

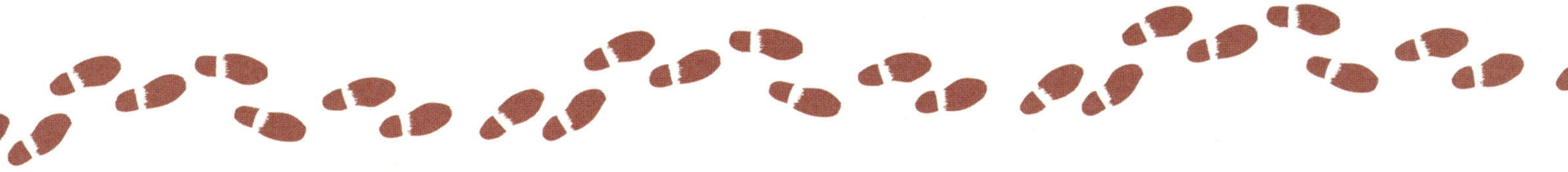

the members of the group were so thirsty that they licked their own sweat, and a couple of the men even drank their own urine. No one wanted to risk eating a snake in case it was poisonous, but eventually things got so bad that they had no choice.

Shortly afterwards two of Gliński's fellow Poles fell ill. They died within hours of each other and were buried side-by-side beneath a pile of stones. The third then seems to have perished somewhere in the Himalayas, the world's highest mountain range, which the remaining four men had to cross to reach the safety of India.

Gliński's recollections of how they did this were vague and confusing. Unfortunately, by the time the four survivors were picked up by soldiers belonging to a British Gurkha regiment, he too was ill, and growing weaker by the day. But even without knowing the details, the most remarkable thing about this escape from Siberia is that four men had somehow survived such a perilous eleven-month journey to reach India and find freedom. That and the fact that one of them, Gliński himself, recovered and was able to rejoin his unit and continue fighting until the end of the war.

Bob Hodges

Printing with a Potato (France, 1941)

Bob Hodges joined the Royal Air Force straight from school and had successfully qualified as a bomber pilot by the time Britain and Germany went to war in September 1939.

Almost exactly a year later his Handley Page Hampden was running out of fuel as he neared the end of a long, nine-hour mission. Hodges knew he didn't have enough in the tanks to make it back to his squadron in Suffolk and was about to attempt an emergency landing in a field when the aircraft came under attack. Moments after the first shell struck, both engines stopped working, and as Hodges wrestled with the controls, trying to restart them, he ordered the crew to bail out.

Two of them successfully parachuted down to the ground, but the third man hadn't heard the order. As a result, Hodges and air gunner Sergeant Wyatt were still in the Hampden when it smashed into the ground and skidded to a halt. Both survived the impact but were now trapped in a part of northern France which had been overrun by enemy troops.

The two men who had parachuted out of the aircraft had been taken prisoner almost immediately. Hodges and Wyatt knew they had to get away as quickly as possible, but first they set light to the aircraft to destroy it, along with some secret documents that they had been carrying on board.

The main danger to them came from German police and soldiers, and also from collaborators, French men and women who had chosen to assist the invaders. Fortunately, there were other citizens who were prepared to risk their own lives to see Germany defeated. Some joined the Resistance, the name given to the groups who continued to attack German troops and facilities even after the French government had surrendered; others did whatever they could to help or hide airmen and those who had become stranded behind enemy lines.

Hodges and Wyatt knew they would have to rely on people like these once they had got away from the crash site on foot. An escape across the heavily guarded English Channel was impossible, so their best chance was to head for the port at Marseilles, even though this was hundreds of kilometres away in the south of France.

Travelling cross-country, from village to village and farm to farm, they were grateful to be given items of French clothing to wear over their uniforms, shoes to stop them being identified by their RAF boots and even an illegal map to help them find the safest route down to Marseilles. Once they spent the night in a large country house owned by a Frenchwoman who was married to an Englishman, while ordinary villagers gave them food to eat on their journey.

This help was invaluable and enabled the pair to stay on the run for about a month, before they reached the town of Luchon, where, unfortunately, they were identified and arrested. Both were taken to another country house, where they were held captive until, on 8 October, Hodges and several other British inmates were transferred to a prison located right by the harbour in Marseilles.

Looking around it, Hodges could see that security at the old-fashioned Fort St Jean prison was not very good at all. It didn't take him long to find a way out, and he then managed to smuggle himself on to a ship that was about to sail to North Africa. Hodges wanted to get to Casablanca in Morocco because he had heard of other pilots finding a way back to Britain from there. Unfortunately, his hiding place was discovered when the vessel docked at the Algerian port of Oran. He was handcuffed, taken off and put on a ship that was sailing back to France.

Hodges was now classified by the enemy as a high escape risk, so he was taken to a third prison that was further inland at Nîmes. This one was called St Hippolyte-du-Fort, and it had a reputation for being much more secure than the old one in Marseilles. Hodges still managed to get out, however, this time with the help of schoolfriend of his from London who happened to be in the same prison.

Remarkably, Hodges escaped using a fake pass that appeared to give him permission to leave the prison for five days. The whole thing sounds unlikely even now, especially as the official-looking stamp in the pass was also fake and had been made in a prison cell using

a carved potato dipped in home-made ink. It was good enough to fool the guards, though, and waving the pass at them, Hodges simply walked out of the supposedly secure jail and disappeared down the street.

He was still more than a thousand kilometres from home, however, and once again members of the Resistance came to his rescue. Hodges was able to make contact with one of its finest secret agents, a woman called Nancy Wake (see p. 131). To the fury of the Gestapo, Germany's secret police, Wake spent several years helping refugees to escape from France, together with hundreds of pilots like Hodges who had been shot down.

With her expert knowledge and assistance Hodges managed to reach the Pyrenees, a vast mountain range on the border between France and Spain. Once over the mountains and in Spain he should have been safe, as it was a neutral country with no official involvement in the war. However, many Spanish people supported Germany's Adolf Hitler, and this meant they didn't want Allied pilots and aircrew using their country as an escape route. They had Hodges arrested and locked up yet again, first in a detention centre and then in Miranda del Ebro, which was one of the country's most feared prisons.

Fortunately, the government in London had begun sending diplomats to Spain who worked hard to get British prisoners like Hodges out of Miranda del Ebro. Skilled pilots were desperately needed if the RAF were to continue fighting, and after more than a month of careful negotiation, it was agreed that Bob Hodges could be released.

He reached England in June 1941, almost eight months after his Hampden had crashed into a French field. Like other pilots who were shot down but uninjured, he immediately returned to duty and went on to fly many more successful missions over the next four years. After the war he was made president of the Royal Air Force Escapers' Society, and in 1968 he was knighted by Queen Elizabeth II.

Charlie Bowden

Bootlaces and Blankets (Greece, 1941)

When thousands of heavily armed German paratroopers landed on the Mediterranean island of Crete in May 1941, it was the start of the first successful airborne invasion in history. The British had been determined to hold on to the island, and believed they could do it with the support of troops from Australia and New Zealand (known as ANZACs) and hundreds of courageous Greek volunteers. Unfortunately, their optimism was misplaced. After only a few days of ferocious fighting it became clear that the Germans were going to win and that the island would soon be under enemy control.

Charlie Bowden was sick and lying in a military-hospital tent when the invasion began. The first the Royal Marine sergeant knew about it was when machine-gun bullets started ripping through the canvas walls of the tent. Shortly afterwards he and several other sick and wounded men were told, in German, that they were now prisoners of war and then marched off in their hospital pyjamas.

Their guards had taken them only a few kilometres when the prisoners came under attack once again. As Bowden ducked for cover, he realised that they were being fired on by their own side. The attackers were New Zealanders, mostly young soldiers on patrol who had mistaken them for enemy troops, despite the fact that they were wearing pyjamas. The chaos caused by the New Zealanders' confusion gave Bowden the chance he was looking for. Making a sudden run for it, he managed to reach the relative safety of a cave overlooking a nearby beach.

He knew he couldn't stay in hiding for long, though, not without food, a weapon of some sort and proper clothing. By now the surrounding countryside was crawling with German soldiers, so it probably wouldn't be long before he was seen and recaptured. Bowden felt sure some of his comrades were still in the area, however, so when the coast was clear he scrambled out of the cave and began looking for them. Fortunately, it didn't take him very long to find a group of Royal Marines, although as he approached them he was shot at again – this time by a British sentry who had also failed to spot his pyjamas.

Once the sergeant had been recognised, however, he was given a replacement uniform and a rifle so he could join a fighting platoon commanded by Major Ralph Garrett. He and his comrades fought bravely for the next four days, but they were heavily outnumbered and half were killed or wounded. It soon became clear that the invasion was succeeding, and knowing that Crete would soon be in enemy hands, Garrett offered the survivors a simple choice: throw down your weapons and surrender or try and find a way off the island.

Garrett decided to go for the second option, although he knew it was very risky. It was clear that help wasn't on its way because most of the British and their allies had already begun retreating from the island. More than thirty RAF aircraft had been lost in the fighting and nineteen ships sunk off the coast. As the aircraft carrier HMS *Formidable* had been badly damaged, along with a submarine and twenty other warships, there was almost no chance of them being rescued by the Royal Navy.

In such desperate circumstances, the discovery of an abandoned landing craft seemed to offer the men their only hope of survival. As their name suggests, landing craft were designed to carry groups of soldiers the short distance from a warship to dry land. Most of them were small, slow and unarmed, and while their flat-bottomed hulls made them perfect for beach landings, they were entirely unsuited to a long sea voyage.

The one that had been abandoned wasn't in very good condition either. Only one of its engines still worked, and there was almost no fuel left in its tanks. With almost 140 anxious men clambering on to it, the whole thing was in serious danger of capsizing as soon as it set off. Their nearest safe harbour was a British base in Egypt that was more than 600 kilometres away. Without adequate supplies of food and drinking water, Bowden can't have been the only one on board who wondered if they would actually make it.

Garrett felt the men had no other option unless they wanted to surrender, and on 1 June the landing craft put to sea, with everyone on board simply hoping for the best. These vessels don't have any cabins, so it was a case of 'standing room only', and the single navigational aid they had was an old map, which, unhelpfully, had all the place names written in Greek. Someone had discovered a few unopened packets of biscuits on the beach, along with some tins of corned beef (known as 'bully'), but there was nowhere near enough of either to last the journey.

The food could be rationed at least, but the fuel was bound to run out, even with only one engine running. When it did, Garrett and Bowden ordered the men to surrender their bootlaces, which they used to stitch some old army blankets into basic sails. This imaginative solution meant the vessel could continue inching its way towards Egypt, but only very slowly and with the fittest men taking turns to steer it by swimming alongside the battered hull.

In this way the vessel took nine days to reach Egypt, although by the time the incredible journey was over, two of the men had died, possibly of their wounds or perhaps due to sunstroke. Even once the survivors had struggled on to the beach, it was impossible to know if they were safe or still in danger. No one could tell in the dark whether they had landed behind British or enemy lines, and the Greek map was completely useless now they were in North Africa.

Bowden and a young Australian officer immediately set off to find out, while some of the other men went looking for fresh water. An emergency fuel pipeline led the pair straight to an army camp close to the town of Sidi Barrani, and luckily it was under British control. As soon as Bowden and the Australian managed to convince the sentries they were on the same side, a convoy of trucks was organised to bring Major Garrett and his near-starving crew to safety. Crete may have been lost (the Germans on the island didn't surrender until 1945), but against all the odds the landing craft had done its job.

Airey Neave

Escape from Colditz Castle (Germany, 1942)

The countries fighting World War II built hundreds of prisoner-of-war camps to accommodate millions of captured soldiers, sailors and airmen. The most famous was Colditz Castle in north-eastern Germany, which the Germans called Oflag IV-C. They believed it to be the most secure in Europe.

A POW camp was often just a collection of large wooden huts surrounded by a barbed-wire fence, but Colditz was very different. It was a thousand-year-old fortress with tall towers and stone walls that were more than two metres thick. The castle had many more armed guards than other POW camps, and its position on a high cliff overlooking the dangerous Zwickauer Mulde river made it seem impregnable.

As the Germans were so sure that its remote location made it escape-proof, for much of the war Colditz was reserved only for very special prisoners. The inmates included several important, high-status individuals, such as the nephews of British Prime Minister Winston

Churchill and King George VI. The actor who played 'Q' in many of the early James Bond films was another prisoner, and POWs who had already tried to escape from other camps in Germany were also sent to Colditz to stop them from having another go.

Unfortunately, this last idea turned out to be a bad one because British and Commonwealth POWs seemed to be much better than German POWs at escaping from prison camps. In nearly six years of fighting not a single German managed to escape from Britain, but approximately 1,200 prisoners escaped from camps in mainland Europe and made it back home. Putting so many of them in one place helped turn Colditz into a sort of school for escapology experts.

Prisoners who had tried to escape once were far more likely to do it again, and for many of them it became a bit of a game. At least one British escapee tried ten times before he was successful. Planning a new escape helped men like him to beat the boredom of being locked up all day. Other prisoners enjoyed the fact that their activities really annoyed the officers and guards who ran Oflag IV-C.

POWs who had gone 'over the wire' but then been recaptured were always happy to share their experiences and expertise with the other inmates. This way hundreds of prisoners quickly learned what worked and what didn't. By cooperating with each other, they were also able to devise new ideas and techniques that could be tested each time yet another escape attempt was made.

Secret workshops were set up in hidden corners of the castle to help them. Inmates' old uniforms were converted to look like German ones or even ordinary civilian clothing. Skilled prisoners copied out maps of Germany by hand or produced fake identity documents for officers who were planning to escape. Others worked turning scraps of metal into useful tools or keys to fit the castle's many locked doors. The most extraordinary creation to come out of these workshops was a full-size working glider, although the war ended before this could be launched from the roof and flown over the walls and across the Zwickauer Mulde.

Admittedly, most escape attempts were not quite this spectacular, and inevitably an awful lot of them failed. However, many of the prisoners made their way out of Germany's supposedly escape-proof castle, and dozens of them managed to reach Britain without being caught. This was called 'doing a home run', and the first to achieve it was a daring young Royal Artillery officer from Essex called Airey Neave. Neave had been wounded in May 1940 and imprisoned, but then escaped shortly afterwards, only to be recaptured before he could get away. The Germans weren't taking any chances with him after that. Thousands of police and army personnel had already wasted so much time chasing escapees like Neave around the country that he was sent to Colditz, where it was hoped he would behave himself.

Neave had no intention of doing this, though, and he made his next escape attempt just weeks after arriving at the castle. He had noticed that some of the prisoners liked to put on little plays to entertain each other. Neave asked to borrow some theatre paint from one of them and used this to make an old Polish uniform he'd found look like a proper German one.

He was quite pleased with the result at first, but unfortunately his ingenious trick didn't work once he got outside. The uniform turned a very strange colour under the castle's security lights, and despite his disguise Neave was quickly spotted as he tried to march out through the main gate while looking like a guard. He was immediately ordered back at gunpoint. Although he was punished by a furious German officer, and even threatened with execution, he was determined to have another go as soon as he could.

His chance came one night in January 1942. He and a Dutch soldier called Anthony Luteyn decided they would make a break for it, despite the viciously cold winter weather. Both men were dressed in three layers of clothes, as they had fake German uniforms and home-made civilian clothes underneath their usual uniforms. Their escape route began with a trapdoor under the stage where the prisoners put on their plays. Beneath this was a narrow passage that led to one of the castle's towers. From there they crept downstairs to the guardroom, after first stripping off their top layer of clothes to reveal the imitation German officers' uniforms they had on underneath.

Neave thought their new disguises were more convincing than his first attempt with the paint. However, he didn't know he was right until the pair entered the guardroom, where several German soldiers stopped and saluted them! After this they made their way outside into the snow but were careful to avoid the main gate, where Neave had been caught before. No one could go through it without the right documents, and neither man had any. Instead, Neave and Luteyn headed for a length of wall that appeared to be less well guarded than the rest of the castle. They clambered over it without being seen and then took off another layer so that they now looked like civilians. They buried their uniforms as quickly as they could to give them as much time as possible to get away before their escape was noticed and the inevitable manhunt began.

Both men had decided to head for Switzerland. This was at least 650 kilometres from the castle, but it was a neutral country where they ought to be safe. Unfortunately, when they tried to buy a couple of train tickets, the woman selling them became suspicious and called the police, who arrested them. Neave and Luteyn protested, saying they were Dutch workers, and then fled when the policeman (who wasn't sure he believed them) went off to check out their story.

They made their escape on foot but were forced to hide several times after encountering groups of Germans who suspected they were escaped prisoners. One night they had to hide out in a derelict garden shed that was so cold their boots froze to the ground. Neave found the only way he could free them was by breathing on the boots to warm them up. Only then could the pair continue their slow and uncomfortable journey south-west.

Altogether it took them nearly four days to reach the border, with almost nothing to eat except a couple of squares of chocolate and nothing to drink except melted snow. Both men were exhausted by the end of it and used their last reserves of energy to sprint over the border.

They split up in Switzerland after shaking hands and wishing each other good luck, as Luteyn wanted to join the Dutch East Indies army in Asia. Neave eventually reached England after spending several weeks travelling through France and Spain to Gibraltar, where he knew he could board a ship home.

As the first British officer to make it back from Colditz, he was made a special agent for MI9, where he remained for the rest of the war. This was a small, highly secret branch of Military Intelligence that helped other prisoners of war escape, as well as thousands of parachutists and airmen who had become stranded behind enemy lines.

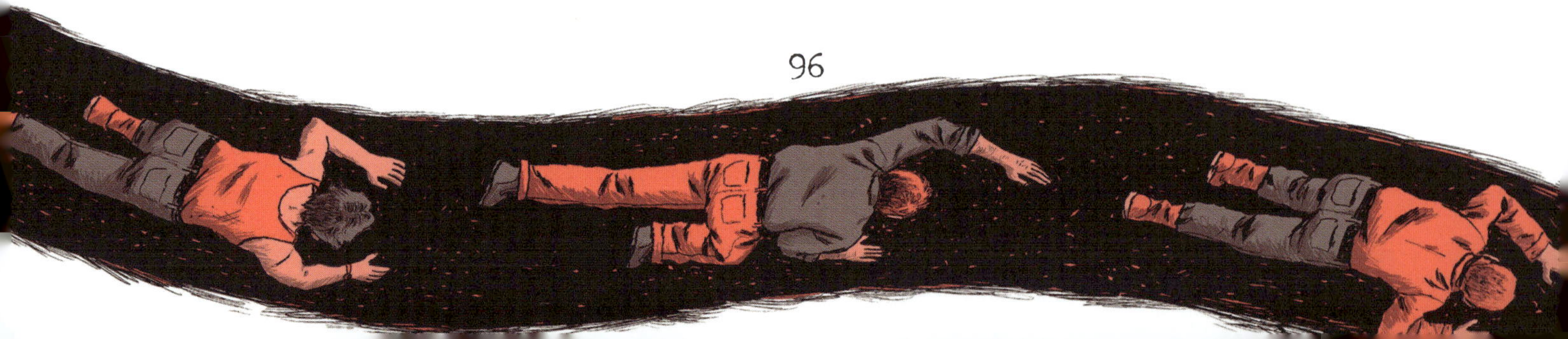

MAP

'Clutty' Hutton

Gadgets Galore (Britain, 1942)

Any prisoner who is planning an escape needs to be resourceful and inventive, as well as very lucky. During World War II, one French general, Henri Giraud, spent two years teaching himself to speak German, as well as memorising maps of the area around the prison where he was being held and knitting together nearly 50 metres of strong rope, which was made from stolen twine, bedsheets torn into strips and copper wire. Giraud used it to lower himself down the walls of Königstein Castle in eastern Germany. He got away, but the British authorities could see that most POWs didn't have this level of ingenuity and would need some extra help if their own attempts were to be as successful as Giraud's.

The War Office in London was keen to assist and established the MI9 department mentioned in the previous chapter, whose staff were specialists in what was called 'escape and evasion'. They spent their time devising ways to help POWs get out of captivity and teaching pilots, spies and other personnel the techniques they needed to avoid being caught if they became trapped behind enemy lines after going on a mission. The results

were spectacular: although MI9 was a very small organisation, it helped around 5,000 men and women to get back to Britain. Most of them escaped from France and Belgium after those countries had been invaded by Germany.

Much of MI9's success depended on the extraordinary gadgets it developed to assist would-be escapees. Many were thought up by a brilliant inventor known as 'Clutty', and they give us a fascinating insight into the secret world of covert warfare and what we now call 'special ops'.

Clutty was a pilot from Birmingham whose real name was Christopher Hutton. He had served in both the army and the air force during World War I, and became interested in inventing things after meeting a famous stage magician and escape artist called Harry Houdini. Clutty was an eccentric, and hopeless when it came to obeying army rules and regulations. However, he was also clever and highly imaginative, and so in 1940 he was asked to join MI9. At that time the organisation was based in a luxury hotel near Trafalgar Square in London, but Clutty soon went off to an underground bunker in the countryside, because he preferred working on his own and didn't like to be disturbed.

During his time at MI9 he invented dozens of ingenious gizmos and gadgets in his underground workshop. MI9 made sure these were carried by men and women going on overseas missions and smuggled thousands of others into prison camps around Europe and Asia. Anything that could help an inmate escape had to be hidden from the guards, and of

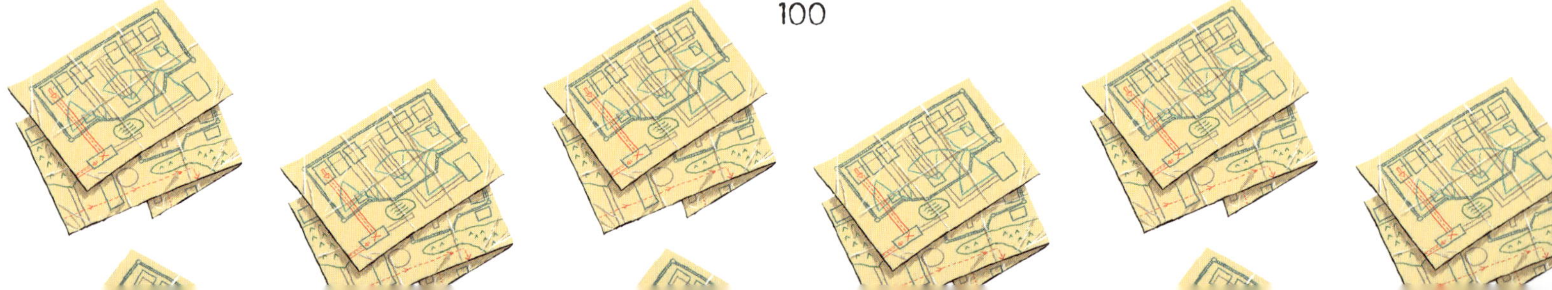

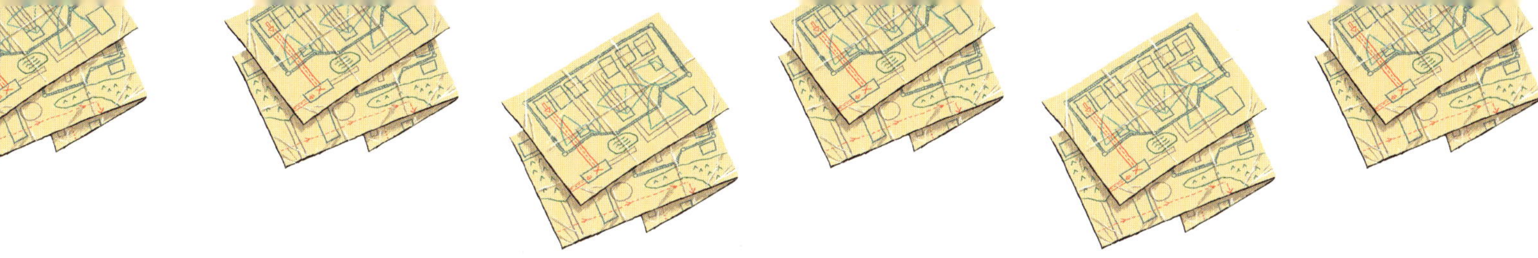

course anyone captured by the enemy was bound to be thoroughly searched. Because of this Clutty spent a lot of his time making these gadgets as tiny as possible or disguising them to look like something completely different.

His magnetic compasses are a good example of this. One was so small it could be hidden inside a false tooth, while others were attached to buttons on military uniforms or concealed in pens and pencils. His compasses were so useful for travelling through enemy territory that more than two million were issued to British and Commonwealth troops over the next few years. Clutty also devised a special magnetised razor blade, which a stranded pilot could use to find north in an emergency.

Even the best compass isn't much use without a map, however, but maps were often the first things to be confiscated when a soldier or airman was arrested. Also, ordinary paper maps would fall apart if an aeroplane had to ditch in the sea, so Clutty began looking for materials that could survive getting wet and be folded up small enough to escape detection.

Clutty's first idea was to print them on very thin silk squares, using a special kind of ink that he had invented himself. The printing was often done on both sides (Germany on one, France on the other), and tests in his workshop showed these maps could still be read after being scrunched up and soaked in seawater. MI9 was delighted with them, and before long British fighter pilots and bomber crews began hiding copies of Clutty's map in their uniforms before taking off on a raid.

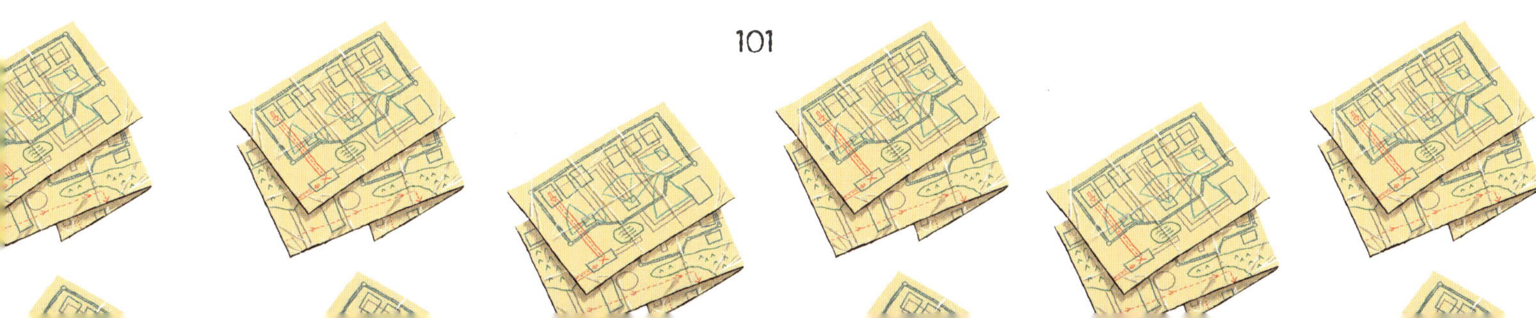

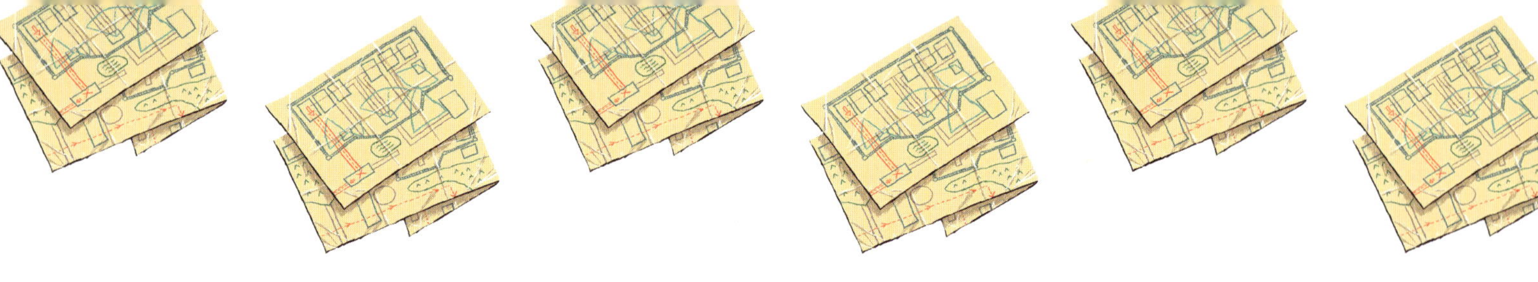

A second type of map was printed on special paper made from the leaves of a mulberry tree. This was so thin that entire maps could be hidden between the front and back of a single playing card or inside a hollow chess piece. These and other games were sent overseas to stop POWs becoming bored, and Clutty's looked so much like the real thing that prison guards didn't bother inspecting them very closely.

A sharp saw was another useful tool for a would-be escapee, and Clutty produced several different types. One was designed to be hidden down a soldier's trouser leg, yet was strong enough to cut through the metal bars of a prison cell. Another was the gigli, a type of flexible blade made of sharp-edged wire. Clutty didn't invent it, but he found a new use for the gigli that no one had thought of before. Giglis are thin enough to hide inside shoelaces, so Clutty suggested concealing them there and using the blades to modify the warm flying boots worn by RAF aircrew: cutting the tops off with a Gigli made them look more like ordinary shoes – a useful trick if a pilot got shot down and needed to disguise himself as a French or Belgian farmworker. Clutty also fitted the boots with hollow heels, which were perfect for hiding tiny compasses in or even a supply of foreign banknotes.

Clothing was often a problem for a man or woman on the run because their British uniform made them extremely easy to identify. MI9 had realised this early on in the war and asked Clutty to come up with a solution. The result was a special type of blanket that could be cut up and stitched to look like an ordinary suit or overcoat. The blankets were included in

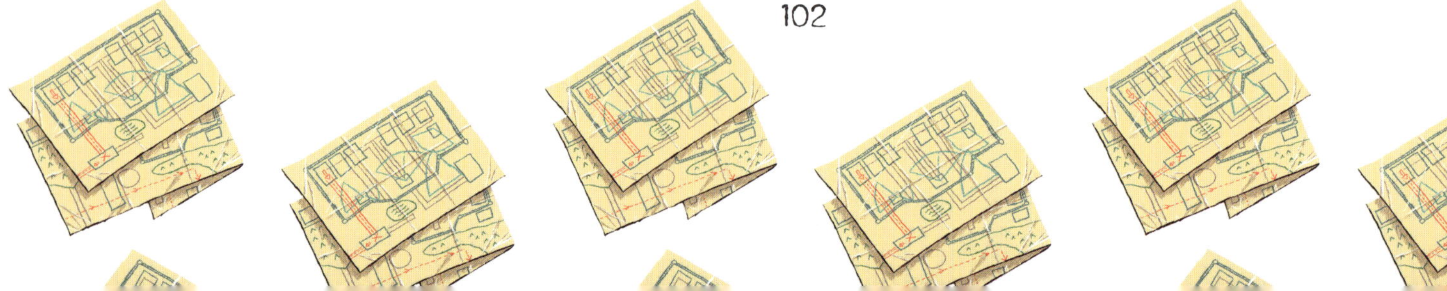

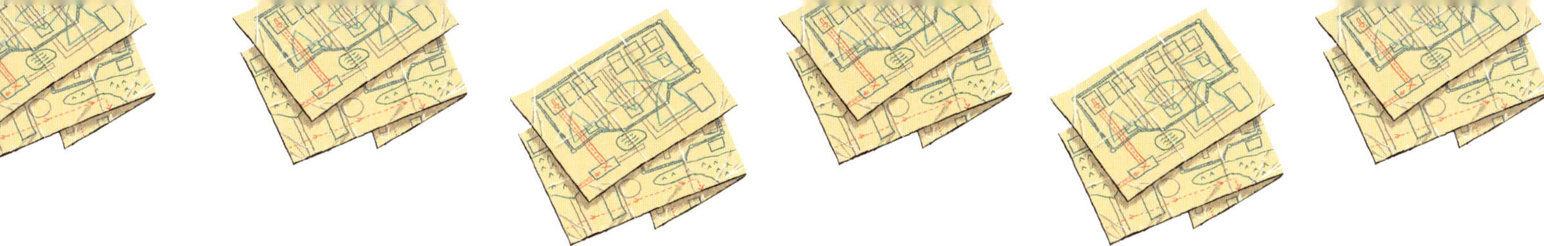

aid packages sent to prisoners. Because most of them weren't trained tailors, Clutty printed instructions on each blanket, which could only be seen once the prisoner had washed it for the first time.

The blankets could also be dyed different colours using a special fountain pen that Clutty had also designed in his workshop. This looked and worked like an ordinary pen but had an ink refill that was divided into three compartments. Two were full of dye, but the top one contained just enough ink to convince a suspicious guard that it was a genuine working pen.

The pen was typical of Clutty's inventions, which were always imaginative, clever and expertly made. A few of them might sound a bit simple now, but they worked brilliantly, and after the war several captured German officers admitted that Clutty and MI9 had made their jobs much, much harder.

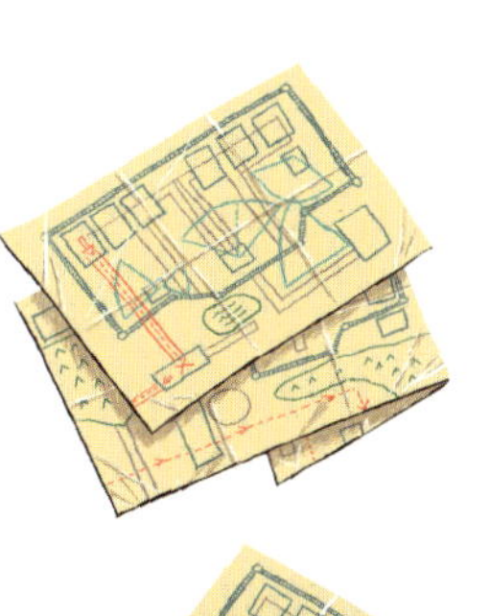

Susan Travers

The First Woman in the French Foreign Legion (Libya, 1942)

The French Foreign Legion is widely recognised as one of the toughest, best-trained and most effective fighting units anywhere in the world. Soldiers from many different countries join it, and for nearly 200 years the volunteers were all fit young men, except for one quiet but courageous Londoner called Susan Travers.

Travers always said she found family life dull and that what she wanted was adventure and excitement, so she signed up as a battlefield ambulance driver at the start of World War II and was sent to Finland. The country had been invaded by Russian troops, but she returned to London in 1940 after learning that France had surrendered to the German army.

London was home to an organisation called the Free French. This was a group of men and women who were determined to continue the fight to liberate their country. Travers was keen to help them, despite not being French. As she could speak the language well,

she decided to join their struggle, although she knew that doing so might be dangerous. Unfortunately, at this time most European countries still refused to let women fight on the front line. Travers was allowed to accompany the Free French troops to North Africa but was given the job of driving senior army officers around a region known as the Western Desert.

This part of the Sahara Desert covers more than half a million square kilometres of Libya and Egypt. The temperature there often reaches 50°C or more, and it was the setting for some of the fiercest fighting of the entire war. Travers quickly found the kind of adventure and excitement she'd been looking for, as much of her time was spent dodging enemy gunfire and finding a route through minefields with her boss, Colonel Koenig of the French Foreign Legion.

In May 1942 Koenig was ordered to defend the remote desert fortress of Bir Hakeim. Travers went with him but must have known it was a hopeless task. The fort itself was hundreds of years old (it even had its own ancient Roman well), and the attacking forces were much more numerous than Koenig's. They were also led by one of Germany's most successful military commanders, Erwin Rommel.

Rommel's skill and cunning in battle were well known and had earned him the nickname of the 'Desert Fox'. His troops had many more tanks, artillery and anti-tank weapons than the fort's defenders, and the French knew that Rommel's ability to organise devastating

surprise attacks had already helped his elite Afrika Korps win several important battles.

The German commander arranged for more than a hundred aircraft to attack the fort dozens of times, including repeated raids by terrifying Stuka dive-bombers. The pilots would be able to pound the old walls into dust, so Koenig ordered all the women to leave the fort while it was still possible for them to escape. Travers refused to obey his order, however, the only female to do so. Instead, she hunkered down with the men in their trenches as one of the worst, most destructive sieges of the desert war began.

Rommel seemed confident of success, even though his Italian allies had failed to capture the fort after several weeks of fierce fighting. His troops with their Panzer tanks, aircraft and heavy artillery ought to have defeated Koenig's force of 3,000 men in a few hours. But, somehow, the Legion managed to cling on, and for more than two weeks they mounted a heroic defence against a much stronger enemy, before running out of food, ammunition and eventually even drinking water.

By midnight on 10 June Koenig knew he was beaten and that the Legion had no alternative but to abandon Bir Hakeim. Travers led the escape by driving Koenig in his Ford car as fast as she could through several lines of German tanks and across the lethal minefields that surrounded the old fort. Before setting off, the colonel had told her that 'If we go, the others will follow,' and within moments a fleet of Foreign Legion vehicles had

formed a line behind them. To begin with the Germans didn't even realise a mass breakout was taking place, but this changed when one of the French trucks ran over a mine, which exploded noisily.

Rommel's troops immediately opened fire, but Travers knew she had to keep going. With her foot firmly planted on the Ford's accelerator pedal, she and Koenig bounced and bumped their way across the barren desert landscape, with the rest of the convoy following on close behind.

It took several hours for Travers to lead more than 2,500 of her comrades to the safety of the British lines. It was only then that she realised just how much danger she and Koenig had been in. While she'd been focused on finding a route for the others to follow, the car had been hit multiple times. Travers later admitted she had enjoyed driving as fast as she dared through the dark night, even though the car's bodywork had been riddled with nearly a dozen bullet holes and the metal badly scarred by shrapnel from exploding tank shells.

Even this wasn't quite enough excitement and adventure for the young Londoner, however. After Bir Hakeim Travers decided to stay on with the Legion, and as the only female legionnaire she went on to see action in Italy, Germany and France. She was injured at least once (after driving over a mine herself), but fortunately survived the war and afterwards settled in her beloved France.

Susan Travers died there in 2003, aged ninety-four. This meant she lived just long enough to see other young women finally able to join the Legion on the same terms as the men. It had taken more than half a century for this to happen, but she must have been proud that, once again, it was her route that others had followed.

Guy Pease

A Loo Roll to the Rescue (France, 1943)

When Guy Pease was shot down over occupied Europe in September 1943, it wasn't the first time the young RAF pilot had found himself in trouble. A few months earlier some sailors in the Free French navy had rescued the twenty-year-old after he had spent more than six exhausting hours struggling to stay afloat in the chilly waters of the English Channel.

On that occasion his aircraft had caught fire while flying low over the sea. Climbing out of the smoke-filled cockpit, Pease was forced back into it again because the straps of his lifejacket had got tangled up in the controls. He managed to release the straps and then calmly flipped the burning aircraft upside down so he could drop out of it into the waves below. Unfortunately, he ripped his lifejacket during the process and then got separated from the inflatable dinghy that all RAF pilots carried onboard for emergencies just like this one. With his heavy flying suit and boots soon completely waterlogged, Pease had no alternative but to tread water until, very close to death, he was spotted and pulled on to the rescue boat.

By September he was back in action, however, piloting a single-seater Mustang on a mission to destroy a military train near the French city of Rouen. The mission was successful, but as Pease turned for home, eight German Focke-Wulf fighters suddenly swooped down on him and unleashed a deadly storm of explosive cannon shells. Several tore into the body of the Mustang, which crashed into an apple orchard moments later.

Pease was still alive, but he was covered in blood. One side of his body was full of metal fragments – probably pieces of his aircraft, as well as bits of explosive shell – and he'd also broken his arm and smashed the fingers of one hand. His rescuers bandaged him head to toe like an ancient Egyptian mummy before he was carted off to a German military hospital in the city. After several painful operations, all performed without anaesthetic, the patient was locked in a ward and left to recover.

Pease was pleased to find there was another pilot in the next bed, a chatty New Zealander called Malcolm Sutherland. His injuries looked even more serious, as he had lost half of his right leg when his Spitfire came under attack from more than fifty German aircraft. The two quickly became friends, and after a few days Sutherland asked Pease whether he thought it would be possible to escape from the ward. The New Zealander said he was keen to try as soon as possible, because once patients in the hospital began to recover from their injuries, the Germans moved them to a prison-of-war camp, where the security was bound to be much tighter.

Pease thought this sounded like a good plan, so they agreed to try to escape as soon as they could. Sutherland saw an opportunity a few weeks later, after a guard left a bunch of keys on one of the beds when he took Pease to the bathroom. The New Zealander carefully traced the shape of one of the keys on to a piece of toilet paper and then set about making a copy of it, using a nail file and an old metal teaspoon. It took a couple of attempts to get this right, but both men were delighted with the result and decided to try the key out the following night.

Their ward was up on the third floor, and they found that the home-made key fitted one of the windows perfectly. Sutherland used it to unlock the window so that Pease could crawl along a narrow ledge outside to reach the room next door. They had to do this because they were wearing only hospital gowns as their uniforms had been taken away when they arrived at the hospital. Feeling around in the dark, Pease managed to find both of the missing uniforms, as well as three shoes – a pair for himself and one for Sutherland's left foot.

A few nights later, after disguising the uniforms by putting them on inside out, the two men lowered themselves down to the ground using a rope they had made by tying bedsheets and blankets together. This was tricky for a couple of seriously injured men, but especially difficult for Sutherland, who had to strap his crutches on to his back. Pease offered to carry Sutherland's heavy wooden leg, which the hospital had provided after his operation. Once they were both down Sutherland put his leg back on and the pair hobbled as fast as they could across the hospital grounds towards a spiked metal fence nearly three metres high.

After cutting their hands trying to climb it, the men realised the fence was too high. Pease offered to push Sutherland to the top so he could wedge the stump of his missing leg between two of the spikes. The men both thought this was pretty funny, but it meant Sutherland would be able to pull Pease up behind him. This worked, and after jumping down to the other side and fitting the artificial leg back on for a second time, the pair then disappeared into the night.

Unfortunately, they soon discovered that getting out of Rouen was much harder than escaping from the hospital. The two men spent several days walking around the streets, avoiding the police and asking strangers for food and money, without success. Each night they had to sleep rough as they had nowhere to stay, and by the fourth day they were suffering from hunger as well as the biting December cold. On top of that, the wounds on their hands were becoming infected, and when at last a young couple took pity on them and invited them home, both men felt continuing would be impossible. While they enjoyed their first proper meal for ages (and were grateful for the chance to sleep in the warm at last), they gave themselves up the following morning and were taken away by the Gestapo.

Their attempt had failed, but Sutherland was right about the Germans. After a few days in a punishment cell he and Pease were both packed off to a prison-of-war camp more than a thousand kilometres away in eastern Germany. He was also right about Stalag Luft III, which had at least 800 armed guards instead of just a handful like at the hospital. Security in the camp was therefore much tighter, but both men knew they were too seriously injured to risk another escape so far from home. After a few months Sutherland was sent to England to be treated for his wounds, but Pease was forced to spend another year at the camp before being taken to another one much closer to Berlin.

By 1945 the war was nearing its end, so this time he wasn't locked up for long. When the guards at this second camp heard a rumour that the Russian army was on its way, they put down their weapons and fled. No one seemed to know what the prisoners were meant to do, and so, deciding he'd had enough, Pease walked out and kept on walking until he found himself among some friendly US troops. They helped him make it back to England, and he was later reunited with his friend Sutherland. Guy Pease lived to be a hundred and died in December 2022.

Roger Bushell

The Tragedy of Tom, Dick and Harry (Germany, 1944)

The prison camp known as Stalag Luft III in eastern Germany was also the setting for the largest and most ambitious escape attempt of World War II. This ended in disaster for almost everyone who took part in it, but their story was later made into an exciting film called *The Great Escape*, starring some of Hollywood's biggest names.

The camp was run by officers of the Luftwaffe, the German air force, and held more than 10,000 prisoners. Most of them were British and American aircrew, but other inmates came from Canada, Australia and New Zealand, as well as Poland, Lithuania, Czechoslovakia, South Africa, Argentina, Norway, Holland and Belgium.

Stalag Luft III was also one of Germany's most secure prison camps, and not just because it had more guards than any of the others. Prisoners slept in large wooden huts that were raised 60 centimetres off the ground to make it difficult for anyone to tunnel out of the barracks without being seen. Also, the camp was situated in a part of the country that has sandy soil, covered by a top layer of grey mud. Because the soil is yellow, if anyone attempts to dig beneath the dark grey layer, it shows up very clearly. It is also hard to dig very far in this kind of soil without the hole (or an escape tunnel) collapsing in on itself.

The prisoners knew all this, but many were still keen to try and break out. Hundreds of them volunteered to help as soon as a Spitfire pilot called Roger Bushell announced his plans for an escape attempt in early 1943. Bushell wanted to dig three tunnels, which were codenamed 'Tom', 'Dick' and 'Harry'. He didn't think all three were likely to succeed, but was confident that at least one of them would. Apart from anything else, he told his fellow POWs enthusiastically, if the Germans managed to discover one or even two of the tunnels, they'd be so pleased with themselves they wouldn't bother looking for another one.

Bushell also believed it would be possible to smuggle as many as 200 prisoners out of the camp this way, although he understood that digging three long tunnels instead of one would require careful planning and an enormous amount of teamwork. In fact, it's now believed that at least 600 prisoners at the camp were involved in Bushell's scheme, although most of them must have known that they would be left behind.

Work on 'Tom' began first, in a corner of one of the camp buildings that, helpfully, was rather dark. The entrance to 'Dick' was concealed behind a wash-house drain and a secure trapdoor, and 'Harry' was hidden beneath one of the stoves that heated the huts. Each tunnel was only around half a metre wide, but together they would have to stretch several hundred metres to reach the woods outside the camp. All the digging would have to be done by hand using home-made tools, and the only light would come from burning animal fat in old tin cans. Thousands of pieces of wood would be needed to stop the walls and ceilings collapsing, and Bushell proposed stealing these from bedframes, tables and chairs.

Although the tunnels were dug more than nine metres underground, it didn't take long for some of the 'goons' (this was the prisoners' nickname for the guards) to work out that something suspicious was going on. It's possible the plan was betrayed by another prisoner, but at the point when 'Tom' was almost completed, the Germans found it and filled it in. However, just as Bushell had predicted, they were so pleased with the discovery that they didn't look around for the other two.

Work on 'Harry', nevertheless, stopped briefly, just to be on the safe side. The decision was also taken to abandon 'Dick', but 'Harry' was finished soon after digging resumed in January 1944. By March everything was ready, and on the evening of the 24th, after a full year of plotting and digging, 200 POWs from more than a dozen different countries prepared to escape.

Bushell had chosen that night because the Moon was obscured by clouds. This made it darker than usual, which was what the escapees wanted, but things began to go wrong almost immediately. It was one of the coldest nights of the year, and the trapdoor to 'Harry' was frozen shut. This delayed the men's departure by more than an hour, and by the time just seventy-six men had made it through the tunnel, several goons had become suspicious. They began searching all the huts to find out exactly what was going on. When they found the entrance to 'Harry', they blocked it off, thereby ensuring nobody else could use it to escape from the camp.

Bushell had already gone through the tunnel. He managed to board a train with another escaped prisoner, but both of them were spotted and arrested shortly afterwards. Seventy-one others were captured not long after, meaning that only three of the seventy-six got away – a Dutchman and two Norwegians. Seventeen of those who were arrested were returned to Stalag Luft III, while others were imprisoned in Colditz Castle or sent to another camp called Sachsenhausen.

After so much effort, the disappointment of those who had been left behind was immense, but it soon became clear that they were actually the lucky ones. When Germany's leader, Adolf Hitler, found out what had happened at Stalag Luft III, he was determined to have his revenge and to send a warning to all other prisoners of war to not attempt anything similar. Within days, the commandant of Stalag Luft III was fired and fifty of the escapees, including Roger Bushell, were shot dead on Hitler's personal orders.

News of this act of cold-blooded mass murder took several weeks to reach London. When it did, it caused an uproar as the killing of POWs had long been considered a war crime under international law. Because of this, many of the officers responsible for the shootings were arrested and put on trial once Germany had been defeated in 1945. Thirteen of them were executed and the remainder given long prison sentences. A handful of others, regretting their actions, had already killed themselves before the trial began.

Nicholas Alkemade

Just Hold Your Breath and Jump (Germany, 1944)

An extraordinary example of an airman being forced to bail out of a burning aircraft occurred over Germany in March 1944. Englishman Nicholas Alkemade's amazing escape story is also one of the strangest you'll ever read, if only because he was a prisoner of war at the end of it instead of at the start.

Alkemade was a rear gunner on board an Avro Lancaster bomber, one of the most dangerous jobs in the wartime RAF. Bombers are larger than fighters, and even the best ones tend to be slower and less manoeuvrable. This means they can be much easier to shoot down and explains why three-quarters of the pilots and aircrew serving in Bomber Command from 1939 to 1945 were injured, killed or taken prisoner. The total, almost 75,500 young men, compares to just 5,500 who had been flying fighters when they were injured, killed or captured.

Whenever a bomber was attacked, the rear gunner was the least likely to escape unhurt. This wasn't just because the enemy often fired from behind, nor because the rear gunner sat inside a Plexiglas dome that was really little more than a large plastic bubble. These so-called 'tail-end Charlies' were also cut off from their crewmates at the front of the aircraft, and their seats were too cramped for them to wear a parachute. This made it much harder for the gunner to get out of the aircraft in an emergency.

Alkemade's Lancaster was one of more than 800 British and American bombers that were returning from a massive night raid on Berlin when it was hit by gunfire. The attacking Junkers 88 Schnellbomber was much faster and more agile than the Avro, and well armed with powerful cannon as well as machine guns. Within seconds the Lancaster was in flames. Alkemade's dome had been completely destroyed, and the pilot was shouting at everyone to bail out immediately.

Alkemade opened the hatch behind him to reach for his parachute, but he was met by a wall of flames. This blocked his path, the heat from the fire so intense that he could feel the rubber of his oxygen mask beginning to melt; in any case, he could see that the parachute was already beginning to burn.

The airman now knew he had no choice but to jump without it. Obviously, he would be killed by the fall (the Lancaster had been flying at an altitude of more than 5,000 metres when it was hit), but somehow this seemed preferable to burning to death while waiting for

the stricken aircraft to explode or smash into the ground.

In fact, Alkemade's flying suit had caught fire when he opened the hatch and he already had some nasty burns to his face and hands. He was lucky that a rush of adrenaline prevented him from noticing this or feeling any pain. Instead, bravely determined to end this hideous ordeal as quickly as he could, the twenty-two-year-old did a backflip and launched himself into the darkness.

At first he had no sensation at all of falling faster and faster through the cold night air. He could see the stars above him at one point, and he gradually became aware of the drumming sound of some aircraft engines in the distance. Powered by gravity alone, Alkemade must have hit a speed of almost 200 kilometres per hour, but eventually he blacked out. This was probably not long after he thought he heard his own aircraft exploding noisily.

He woke up approximately three hours later and found himself lying in a deep bank of snow. Alkemade was in considerable pain and felt extremely cold, although it didn't take him long to work out that the snow had probably saved his life. In fact, he had fallen through the branches of some tall fir trees before hitting the ground. This had slowed him down, and the shade from the trees had prevented the snow from melting in the spring sunshine, meaning there was just enough of it left to give him a relatively soft landing.

The airman knew at once that he had been extraordinarily lucky. His boots had been ripped off by the speed of his descent, he couldn't stand up and one of his knees definitely felt a bit dodgy. However, he was reasonably sure he had just twisted it rather than breaking any bones, and 50 centimetres of freezing snow was enough to give him some relief from the pain of the burns to his head and hands.

Alkemade began calling out for help and blew loudly on the whistle that RAF airmen carried with them for this sort of emergency. His greatest worry was that he had no idea whether he was in Germany or France, let alone if he was near a village or halfway up a mountain, where no one would hear his cries for help.

Fortunately, somebody did hear the whistle, and shortly afterwards a group of local men arrived to carry him to a nearby hospital. The following day the police were at the hospital in force, demanding to know who this enemy airman was and how he had arrived in their neighbourhood. Alkemade described what had happened to him but, unsurprisingly, no one believed that he had jumped out of a burning aeroplane and survived a 5-kilometre fall without a parachute. A more likely explanation was that he was a spy and had buried his parachute in the snow, and everyone knew that spies in wartime were usually just taken out and shot.

Alkemade, panicking slightly, insisted they look for the parachute first or, better still, find out where the Lancaster had crashed and look for it there. Luckily for him, the wreckage

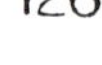

was discovered more than 30 kilometres away. An inspection quickly revealed the charred remains of a parachute near the rear hatch, which meant that, as improbable as it sounded, Alkemade's story must indeed be true.

The Englishman's astonishing survival made him something of a celebrity, both in Germany and later back in Britain. However, there was no question of a captured airman being released, and after three weeks recovering from his injuries in hospital, Alkemade was moved to a prisoner-of-war camp in eastern Germany. He made no attempt to escape and was returned to Britain, fit at last, when the war ended a year later.

Nancy Wake

Running Rings Around the Enemy (France, 1944)

Women of all ages, from teenagers to grey-haired old ladies, volunteered to join the French Resistance during World War II. Many found they had a number of significant advantages over their male comrades, and the most talented ones have gone down in history as some of the most daring and courageous secret agents of the entire war.

Because so many men were away fighting, female members of the Resistance were able to blend in more easily in towns and cities where women and children made up most of the civilian population. Also, at least to begin with, it didn't occur to the enemy that a woman might be working as an agent or saboteur. In the 1930s and 1940s nearly all soldiers, sailors and aircrew were men, so no one expected women to be involved in blowing up trains or helping British and American pilots to avoid being caught after their planes had been shot down.

The Germans eventually worked out what was going on, however, and from then on these fearless female agents faced exactly the same dangers and the same brutality as male ones.

Women like Nancy Wake took enormous risks all the time, and they were forced to escape from one difficult situation or another on an almost daily basis.

Wake had been born in New Zealand but as a young woman moved to France, where she began working as a journalist. She once interviewed Adolf Hitler, and during a visit to Austria was appalled to see his supporters beating up ordinary men and women in the street. By 1940, when France was invaded by the German army, she had married a Frenchman and decided that she would help to defend his country in any way she could.

Her first move was to join one of the small, secretive organisations that smuggled British and Commonwealth military personnel out of German-held territory. She sold her jewellery to provide funds for numerous successful escapes, including one involving Bob Hodges (see p. 81), but organising these escape attempts meant her life was in almost constant danger. Members of organisations like hers risked being tortured and then killed if they were ever caught by the Gestapo. Wake's husband Henri was one of their victims, but her own ability to avoid being captured earned her the nickname of 'White Mouse'. The Gestapo called her this because of the way she seemed to vanish every time they thought they had found out where she was hiding. But it wasn't a friendly nickname. Germany's military police hated her for making them look bad at their jobs and eventually offered a reward of five million francs to anyone who could catch her. In the 1940s this was an enormous amount of money, more than enough to buy a large country house.

Unfortunately, Wake's organisation was betrayed in 1943, when two French traitors managed to join it and then tipped off the Gestapo. She realised she had to get out of France fast, and fled using the same escape routes through the mountains that had been used to save so many airmen and refugees. In all, it took her five attempts before she reached the safety of England, but as soon as she got there she began looking for a way to get back to France.

By this time Britain had its own secret organisation called the Special Operations Executive, or SOE. This was based in London and specialised in getting undercover agents into countries occupied by Germany's armed forces, either by submarine or by using specially adapted aircraft. SOE agents in France worked hard to support members of the Resistance, supplying them with guns, ammunition and money, and showing them the most effective ways to blow up the railway lines, factories and other buildings used by the invading army.

Wake volunteered for it straightaway, and after specialist training she was dropped by parachute into France. To the SOE she must have seemed like the perfect secret agent: she spoke French fluently, was courageous and tough, and already knew how the German military liked to work. She was also a good shot, one of SOE's best, and on at least one mission she silenced an enemy sentry with a karate chop to the neck to stop him raising the alarm. Before long she was organising more than 8,000 members of the Resistance and leading devastating attacks on German military targets.

It was during one of these missions that the White Mouse pulled off her most remarkable disappearing trick. She had escaped once before by jumping from a fast-moving train, and in 1944, while cycling hundreds of kilometres through enemy territory, Wake managed to give the Germans the slip multiple times over the course of several days.

The long journey was necessary to reach a working radio set and the secret codebooks the Resistance needed to communicate with the SOE in London. It involved her cycling approximately 500 kilometres through numerous German roadblocks, each of which was patrolled by armed guards. Completing it took more than seventy hours (equivalent to three days and three nights), and Wake had to sleep rough each night, in ditches or under a hedge. Every morning she had to make sure that her clothes looked neat and clean; that way, if she was stopped at a roadblock, the guards manning it would think she had just nipped out to do some shopping or was visiting a friend.

The ruse worked perfectly, but Wake was completely exhausted at the end of her ordeal and later admitted, 'I couldn't stand up, I couldn't sit down. I couldn't do anything. I just cried.' As for the Germans, who had more than 20,000 troops in the area looking for her, they simply couldn't believe that the White Mouse had managed to escape yet again.

At the end of the war Nancy Wake was awarded the George Medal, one of Britain's highest civilian decorations, and recognised with similar honours by the governments of France, Australia and the United States.

Hélène Podliasky

Nine Friends Play Dead on a Death March (Germany, 1945)

In 1945, as Germany began to realise it was losing the war, hundreds of thousands of prisoners were forced to march enormous distances between their prison camps and German cities. Often this was done in an attempt to hide evidence of the mass killings that had taken place at the worst ones. Once the prisoners had been marched away, the buildings were burned down to the ground and trees planted to disguise the sites completely. Other marches were simply a cruel but effective way of ensuring that German factories had enough slave labourers to make the weapons and ammunition Hitler's army needed.

The marches quickly became known as 'death marches' because so many of the prisoners died without ever reaching their destinations. No one knows the exact number of victims, but without enough food and water at least 200,000 men, women and young children collapsed and died on the marches, or were shot or beaten to death by the brutal armed guards who accompanied them on these terrible journeys.

On a cold morning in April 1945, only a month before Germany was defeated, a large group of around 5,000 women were ordered to leave a notorious prison camp called Ravensbrück. It was about 80 kilometres north of Berlin and had been built to house female prisoners from more than two dozen countries. The conditions behind its high wire fences were appalling. Inmates were frequently starved and tortured, or stripped naked and made to stand outside in the snow and freezing rain for hours at a time.

Among the women ordered to march were nine close friends: six were French, two Dutch and one Spanish. They were called Hélène Podliasky, Suzanne Maudet, Nicole Clarence, Jacky Aubéry du Boulley, Madelon Verstijnen, Guillemette Daendels, Renée Lebon Châtenay, Yvonne Le Guillou and Josée Bordanava. All nine had been members of the Resistance in France, before being arrested by the Gestapo and taken to Germany. Most of them were still in their early twenties and had endured vicious punishments before arriving at Ravensbrück, as well as in the camp itself.

During their imprisonment at Ravensbrück the young women had been made to work as slaves in a nearby weapons factory. The decision to move them was made after several bombing raids on the factory, when it looked as though the camp was about to be surrounded by the Russian army. Although their time at Ravensbrück had been horrific, the sudden order to join a march was a terrible blow to all the women.

Many of them were already weakened by years of imprisonment and hunger, and most

had only thin, poor-quality prison clothes and worn-out shoes that were totally unsuited to a long journey on foot. This was certainly true of Podliasky and her friends, several of whom were seriously ill from the diseases that spread rapidly through the dirty, overcrowded camps. They were all determined to stick together as a group, but equally determined to escape as soon as possible after leaving Ravensbrück. The friends knew that if they didn't get away, they would probably die on the march – either by starving to death or because the guards had instructions to shoot anyone who fell behind or looked too weak to keep up.

Podliasky was only twenty-four years old but she was intelligent and quick-thinking, a professor's daughter who spoke five languages fluently, including German. As a result, her friends looked to her as their unofficial leader, so she began looking for a way to escape as soon as they were outside the camp.

It seemed to Podliasky that the march was badly organised, probably because the order to leave the camp had been so sudden. There weren't enough guards to keep a close eye on so many thousands of women, and Podliasky had noticed that although everyone had set off from Ravensbrück at the same time, gaps were opening up in the long line of prisoners since some of the women were shuffling along more slowly than the rest.

Her first idea was to make a run for it as soon as it got dark. She thought maybe the friends could slip away into the forest while the guards closest to them weren't looking. However, she changed her mind when she saw how many dead bodies were lying in ditches or by the

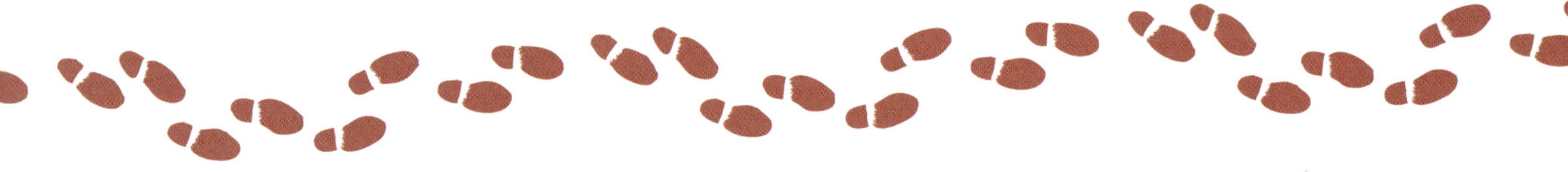

side of the road they were marching along. Some were clearly women who had been shot by the guards or older ones who had collapsed and died of exhaustion; others were the rotting corpses of soldiers, killed days or even weeks before while fighting the war.

The sight of so many dead was shocking, but it gave Podliasky another idea. This one also involved slipping away, but now she was wondering whether they could reach one of the ditches and then hide among the dead bodies until the rest of the prisoners had marched on down the road and disappeared.

The new plan was just as risky as the old one, and horribly gruesome, but it might work, and anyway she and her friends were getting desperate. A woman ahead of them had been shot dead after bending down to pick up a rotten apple, so when Podliasky spotted a bend in the road ahead, she realised it was now or never. She was sure the guards closest to them wouldn't be able to see around the corner, so as they neared the bend, she quickly whispered for the others to follow her and ran towards the nearest ditch. The women all held hands as they jumped into it and then lay among the stinking corpses. Podliasky told them to keep as still as possible for as long as possible. That way, if one of the guards *did* look into the ditch, he might assume the women had been shot by his colleagues near the front of the column and were already dead.

For several minutes the friends lay completely still. Expecting a gunshot at any moment, they were literally too scared to move, but then, her heart thumping madly, Madelon

Verstijnen slowly raised her head. When she looked out, all she could see were feet, hundreds and hundreds of bleeding, blistered feet still marching down the road as if nothing had happened.

Verstijnen ducked down again, and the friends remained hidden until they could no longer hear any sounds from the marchers or their guards. Although no one had seen them jumping into the ditch, the women knew they were still in terrible danger. Countless escaped prisoners just like them had been shot dead by ordinary German citizens or handed over to the police while looking for food and shelter. Because of this, Podliasky realised that their survival depended on them making contact with the American troops who had begun marching into Germany.

Over the course of more than a week the friends slowly made their way towards the front line, eating what little food they could find and snatching a few hours' rest in a ditch or an old barn whenever possible. On the tenth day, Podliasky finally heard a friendly American voice, when a jeep pulled up alongside the women and its driver smiled and offered them a cigarette. At last, the friends knew they were safe.

Harry Deterling

The Train Takes the Strain (Berlin, 1961)

Europe was divided along political lines in the years after the end of World War II. Josef Stalin, Russia's communist dictator, managed to seize control of much of Eastern Europe, and Germany was split into two separate countries. The western half became the Federal Republic of Germany and included all the areas occupied by the British, French and Americans at the end of the war. Next door to this was a new country called the German Democratic Republic. This was established in the territories taken over by Stalin's army.

On the night of 12 August 1961 the communist authorities in the eastern half of Germany decided to close the border between the two territories. The following day they began constructing what became known as the Berlin Wall, a massive barrier of concrete, heavy steel spikes and barbed wire. The 40-kilometre wall divided the city of Berlin in two and, until its demolition in 1989, was intended to stop East Germans escaping to live in the more prosperous West.

This extraordinary move caught everyone by surprise, including many East Germans who were visiting friends and family in West Berlin when the border was suddenly closed. A lot of them simply chose to stay in the West and start a new life there, and over the next twenty-eight years many others began looking for ways to follow them over the wall (or under it) without being shot or arrested by border guards.

The guards were armed and known as Vopos. Around 14,000 of them were stationed along the frontier, so East Germans attempting to escape knew they were taking an enormous risk. Most failed. Tens of thousands of them were caught and punished for trying to leave their own country, and more than a hundred were shot or killed themselves after being arrested near the wall. However, those who were able to get away often showed incredible daring, as well as great ingenuity.

In 1962, for example, an eighty-one-year-old man organised a group of old-age pensioners who managed to dig a 32-metre-long tunnel beneath the border, and the following year a teenager escaped by stealing a Russian tank and ramming it into the wall. In 1965 an office worker set up a zip line on top of the six-storey building where he worked so he could use it to whizz over the wall with his wife and son; several Vopos manning a nearby machine-gun post actually watched them doing it but wrongly assumed that they were East German spies being sent to the West on a top-secret mission! A few years after this a couple of men escaped by hiding inside a giant plastic model of a cow, and in the

1970s two others successfully floated their families to freedom in a hot-air balloon they had made themselves at home.

On that occasion eight people escaped, but a much larger group succeeded after excavating a tunnel that was even longer than the one the pensioners built. This time the work was carried out by a group of youngsters, mostly university students, who spent five months digging beneath the cellar of an abandoned bakery. The work went on twenty-four hours a day, seven days a week, and when it was finished the new tunnel stretched an impressive 145 metres from east to west. Over the course of the next two nights no fewer than fifty-seven people crawled through it to escape, a record that was never broken. Unfortunately, the Vopos became suspicious because so many people were milling around the area. After investigating they made several arrests and then blocked up the entrance. Interestingly, one of the students involved in the escape, Joachim Neumann, got a job in civil engineering after finishing his degree. Over the course of his long career he built more than sixty tunnels for the West German railway system, as well as working on the Channel Tunnel linking England and France.

The success of the Berlin tunnels relied on the diggers staying hidden and keeping quiet, but one of the most famous escapes in the history of the wall was probably also the noisiest. This one was dreamt up by another young engineer, who was employed as a driver on the East German railway network. Like many young people, Harry Deterling was desperate to leave the country as soon as possible. He got his chance on 5 December 1961 (his birthday, as it happened), while driving a train towards Berlin's Albrechtshof station. The station was the last on the line, but instead of slowing down as he reached the platforms, Deterling accelerated hard. Moments later his 100-ton Type 18 locomotive ploughed through several heavy coils of barbed wire and steamed into West Berlin before the border guards had even realised what was happening.

The Vopos weren't the only ones taken by surprise. The people on board included several members of Deterling's own family, but also more than a dozen unsuspecting passengers. They weren't part of the plan at all and had been expecting to get off the train at Albrechtshof. Deterling and his family were clearly delighted to have crossed the border, but these other passengers weren't and at least seven of them went straight back to East Berlin.

The East German authorities were naturally furious and demanded that their locomotive be returned at once. The train was towed back across the border almost immediately, and the following morning the remains of the barbed-wire coils were cleared away and replaced with a new section of solid concrete wall. This remained in place until 1989, when the political situation in Europe improved. The two Germanies were reunited as a single country once again, and the hated wall was finally taken down.

Clarence Anglin, John Anglin and Frank Morris

An Impossible Escape from an Escape-Proof Island (US, 1962)

America's most famous prison was built in the 1930s on a small rocky island in San Francisco Bay. Alcatraz is now a popular tourist attraction, but until it was closed down and its prisoners transferred to other jails in 1963, it had a well-deserved reputation as one of the country's toughest maximum-security prisons.

For many years it was considered escape-proof by the guards who worked there. More than thirty inmates had tried to break out, on fourteen separate occasions, but nearly all of them were caught or died while trying to swim back to the mainland through the cold, shark-infested waters surrounding the rock.

The island's most famous prisoner was a vicious gangster called Al Capone. He spent four and a half years in one of the cell blocks on Alcatraz, and although he didn't try to escape, he did get into a fight with another inmate, who stabbed him with a pair of scissors. Alcatraz was obviously a very dangerous place, even for a powerful crime boss like Capone.

A year before it closed the prison hit the headlines around the world when three prisoners were reported to be missing. Clarence Anglin, his brother John and Frank Morris were violent criminals who were serving long sentences. Each of them had numerous convictions for burglary, bank robbery and other serious crimes, and all three had spent years in various different prisons around the country before ending up at Alcatraz.

On 12 June 1962, while inspecting the cells as they did every morning, the guards discovered that three of them were empty. No one had noticed this during the night because Morris and the Anglins had carefully placed life-sized dummies under their bedclothes. The heads were made of papier mâché, which the men had created by mixing soap, toothpaste, concrete dust and toilet paper. Each one had been painted to make it look like a real person. When the guards patrolled the cell block after dark, it appeared as if the men were fast asleep in their beds. In fact, all three had crawled out of their cells several hours earlier, and thanks to some very careful planning, had managed to find a way out of the main prison building and off the island.

Because none of the men was ever seen again, we only know how they did it because a prisoner in a neighbouring cell later admitted that he had been involved in their escape.

Allen West told the guards that he had wanted to flee with the other three, but after getting trapped in his cell he quickly realised that Morris and the others had gone without him and so went back to sleep.

Over the next few days West described how much thought and planning had gone into the escape. More details about it came from a Federal Bureau of Investigation (FBI) enquiry, which the authorities set up to ensure that nothing similar ever happened again. The FBI agents were convinced that Morris must have been the brains behind the scheme because he was much more intelligent than either of the brothers. Their investigation revealed that the prisoners had managed to remove the ventilation grilles in their cell walls. This had been done by using a hand-operated drill that the men had made themselves. It must have taken many weeks to do this because dozens of tiny holes had to be drilled through the wall to weaken the concrete around each grille.

West had a problem doing this in his cell, which is how he became trapped. However, once they'd removed their grilles, Morris and the Anglins crawled through to a disused corridor that ran behind the cells. The corridor was largely unguarded because it wasn't in regular use, so the men were able to reach the roof, where they had stashed the rest of the equipment they needed to escape. This must have been done over many nights, meaning the men had been leaving their cells after dark and then returning to them before daylight the next day.

As well as using this time to search for a way out, the prisoners had constructed an inflatable rubber raft out of raincoats stolen from the guards. Odd pieces of wood were similarly collected and used to make an oar (or maybe a couple) so that the men could paddle approximately three kilometres to the shore. Having gathered everything together, the FBI think the escapees then found a way down from the roof via a brick chimney stack, before climbing over two high fences to reach the water.

It was, by any standard, a brilliant plan, but unfortunately for the prisoners, there is no evidence that any of them made it safely back to the mainland. After spending weeks searching the prison and the surrounding area the FBI recovered various items associated with the escape. These included an oar, some pieces of rubber raincoat and a packet of letters belonging to one of the escapees. A home-made lifejacket was also found on the nearby Cronkhite Beach, but even here there were no signs of the prisoners themselves.

The waters around Alcatraz are known to be highly dangerous for swimmers, but no bodies were ever found, so it might be possible that at least one of the prisoners made it to a safe beach and then fled inland. However, most people who have studied the escape think this is very unlikely. All three men were career criminals who had offended again and again, and all of them had been arrested multiple times. Even if they had managed to escape from Alcatraz, most experts think they would have been caught shortly afterwards, either while committing yet another crime or while acting suspiciously enough for a member of the public to call the police.

Of course, we can't be sure about this. Nearly six decades on the truth is that no one knows what really happened. Three criminals managed to get out of their cells – several times, in fact – but beyond that the most famous escape in the history of Alcatraz remains a total mystery. Did they reach the mainland and go on to live happy lives? Or did they drown or get eaten by sharks? No one knows, not even the FBI, which spent nearly twenty years looking for evidence. Eventually, even they gave up, so it's probably fair to say that this is one intriguing puzzle that will never be solved.

George Blake

The Spy and the Camper Van (UK, 1966)

A prison or prison-camp roll call was a bit like reading out the register at school each morning to find out who is in class and who is off sick. Prisoners were often lined up outside and required to shout out 'Yes' when their names were called out by one of the guards. Roll calls used to be carried out every day at Wormwood Scrubs prison in west London, but one morning in October 1966 one of the names went unanswered. George Blake, a man convicted of spying for the Russians, had managed to climb over the prison wall and then disappeared.

Blake was actually a British citizen and had already been in prison for five years, after being found guilty of a number of charges relating to treason and espionage. His crimes dated back to the 1950s, when Blake had switched sides and become a communist agent after being captured and held prisoner during the Korean War.

The war had begun in 1950, when communist North Korea invaded South Korea. The invasion was supported by two communist states, China and Russia, while Britain and the

US sided with South Korea. For a while it looked as though it could develop into a third world war, but it ended three years later, and Blake was released, along with many other prisoners.

After returning to London he was employed by the Secret Intelligence Service (known as MI6) because no one realised he had switched sides. Perhaps because his colleagues regarded him as a war hero, none of them had noticed him making illegal copies every time an interesting or top-secret document landed on his desk.

He continued doing this when he was transferred from London to Vienna, Milan and then Berlin. Wherever he was working, he found it was easy to slip away from the office every two or three weeks without being seen. On each occasion he met up with an agent working for the KGB, the Russian secret service, and handed over the copies he had made of the secret documents.

This went on for almost ten years, without anyone in MI6 realising it was happening. It was only in 1961, when Blake was suddenly ordered back to London, that he realised he had been found out. A Polish spy had informed MI6 that Blake was a traitor, and when he reached London he was arrested and told that his time as a double agent was at an end.

The charges against him were extremely serious, but Blake refused to deny his guilt and expected to get a prison sentence of about fourteen years. At the time, fourteen years was

the maximum penalty for spying, but once he was in court, Blake learned that he was to be imprisoned for fourteen years for each of three different crimes. This meant he would serve a total of forty-two years behind bars, a longer sentence than had ever been handed down to a spy before.

The length of his punishment was extraordinary, but so were Blake's crimes. He happily admitted that even he had no idea how many secret documents he had given to the Russians, because there were simply too many of them to count. He also agreed that he had betrayed as many as four hundred of his friends and fellow agents to the KGB. As a result, many of these courageous men and women were never seen again, because they were either executed or imprisoned until they died.

The head of MI6 later declared that Blake's treachery meant he had caused more damage to British intelligence than any other double agent. But despite this, the length of his prison sentence shocked many ordinary members of the public. Three of them were so appalled that they decided to get him out of prison as soon as possible. Irishman Sean Bourke didn't think he was innocent, and neither did his friends Michael Randle and Pat Pottle, but the sentence Blake received seemed so unfair to them that they began hatching a plot to spring him from Wormwood Scrubs and help him to find a way to reach Moscow.

Their plan was carefully thought out but actually extremely simple. More than anything, it relied on the prison being badly run rather than any particular skill or ingenuity. Security

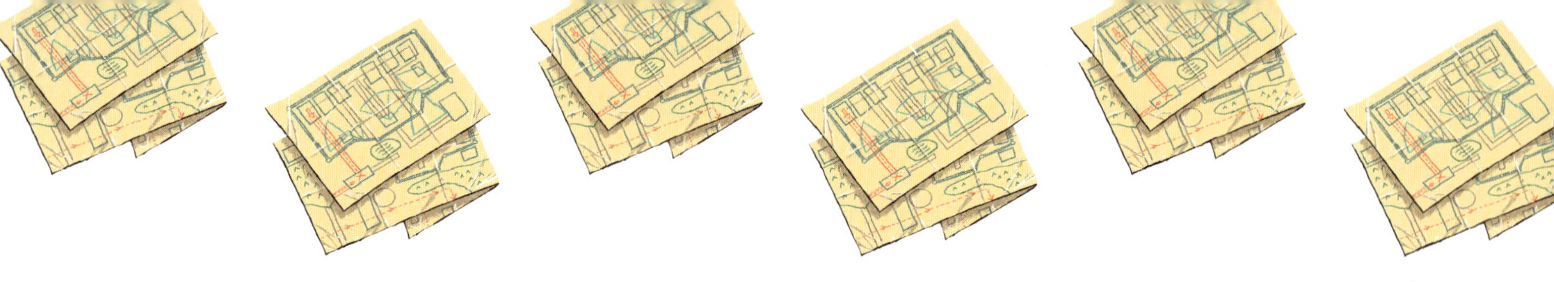

at 'the Scrubs' was so weak that the three conspirators were able to smuggle a walkie-talkie into Blake's cell. They also knew that the former spy was left completely unguarded for most of the time, even though he was the prison's most notorious inmate. Their plan therefore involved little more than throwing a home-made rope ladder over the prison's eastern wall at the right time of day. This was made of string and knitting needles, but it was just about strong enough for Blake to use in order to scale the six-metre-high wall and get out. Once over the wall, he was bundled into a waiting car and driven to the men's secret hideout.

The refuge was only a few hundred metres from the prison, a tiny flat that Bourke had rented after disguising himself with a pair of spectacles (without any lenses) and a pretend beard. The flat's owner was German, which may explain why he didn't spot Bourke's fake English accent, but to be on the safe side, Blake was moved to another flat not long afterwards. While he was there, his three rescuers spent time working out the safest way of getting him out of the country.

Blake wanted to go to East Germany, a country which at the time was under the control of a communist government that supported Russia. By December his liberators had decided that the best way to get there was to cross the English Channel in a ferry bound for Belgium. Blake would need a fake passport for this, so Randle spent some time modifying an old one of his with a new photograph and copies of all the official stamps. Once he had done this, he

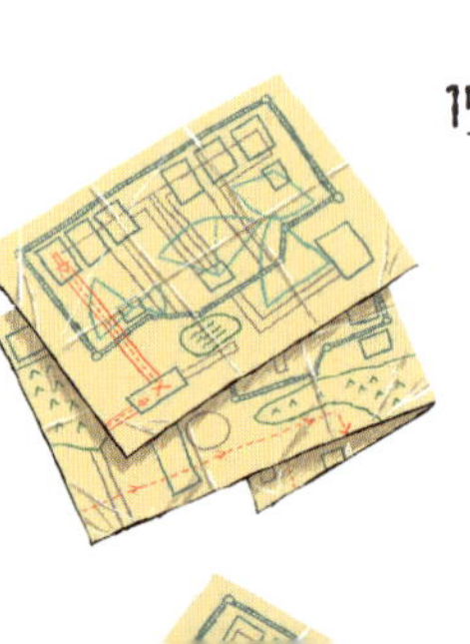

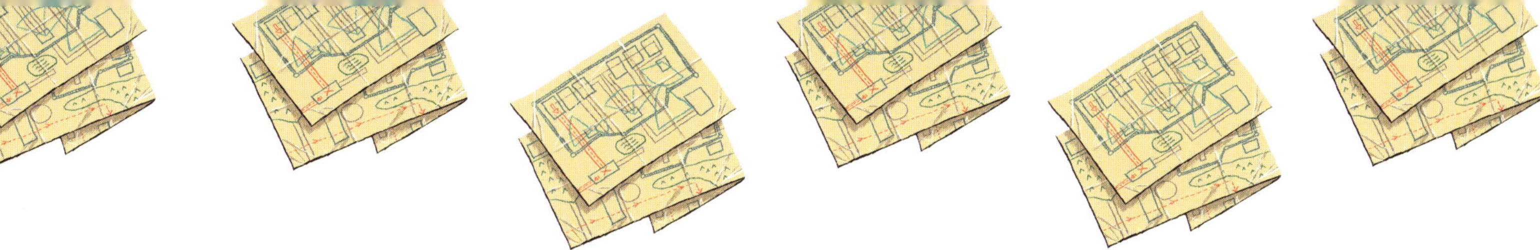

and his wife prepared to drive Blake on to the ship in an old camper van.

This was probably the riskiest part of the plan, even though the camper van had been converted to incorporate a secret compartment that was hidden behind a false drawer. It couldn't be seen through the window of the camper van and was large enough for Blake to hide in for short periods. All the Randles had to do was to drive from the ferry port at Ostend to the East German border and hope nobody stopped them along the way.

By now the men knew that the British authorities were so embarrassed by Blake's escape, and so desperate to catch him, that they were searching almost every vehicle that attempted to leave the country. The newspapers reported that on one occasion, officials had even ordered a coffin to be opened before the vehicle it was in could board the ferry. Because of this, the Randles decided to bring their children along. That way it would look as though the camper van was simply being used for an ordinary family holiday.

Remarkably, this simple trick worked, and the only time an official bothered to inspect the vehicle was when the Randles arrived in East Germany. The inspection was carried out by two friendly East German border guards, but even they didn't look very closely because they didn't want to disturb the children, who had both fallen asleep in the back.

After the guards waved them on, the Randles drove to a hotel where they had agreed to drop off Blake so he could be collected by KGB agents. A few months after that, he was

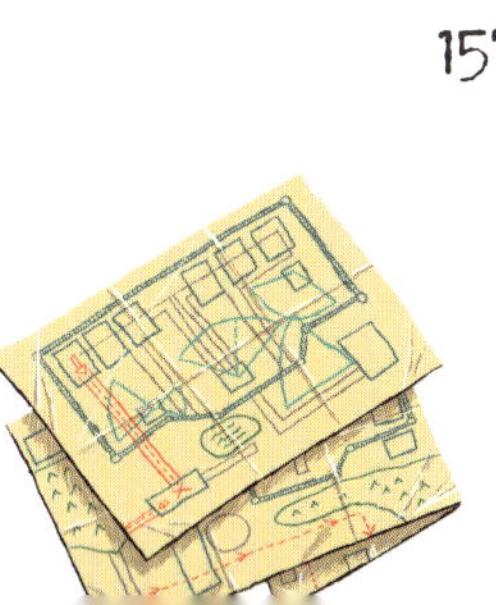
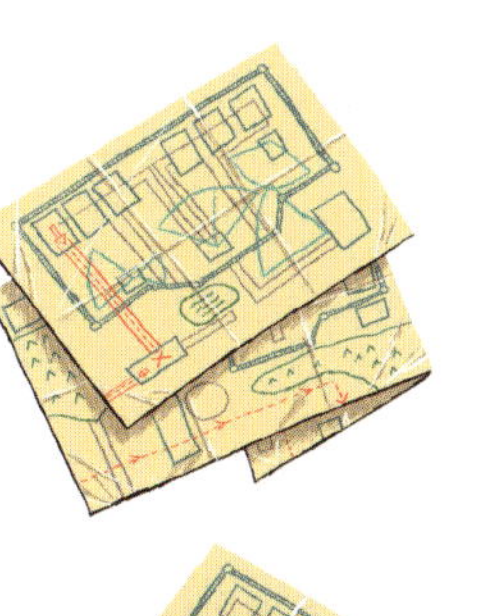

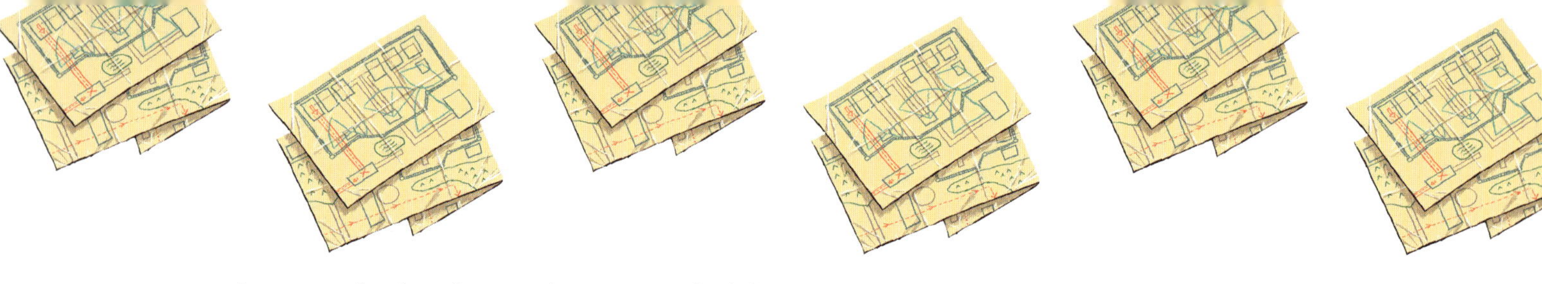

photographed smiling and enjoying a holiday with his mother in the Carpathian Mountains. The KGB was clearly delighted to have its spy back, paying for the vacation and quickly promoting Blake to the rank of colonel. In 2007 President Vladimir Putin presented him with the Order of Friendship, one of Russia's very highest awards. Blake never visited England again and remained in Moscow until 2020, when he died peacefully of old age.

Although Blake's escape was a total success, Pottle and Randle were eventually arrested for their part in it, but only after publishing a book in 1990, in which they described what they had done (Bourke escaped arrest, having died several years earlier). When the pair were brought into court, they defended themselves by saying that although they knew Blake was guilty of some very serious crimes, they thought his enormously long sentence was cruel and inhumane.

Amazingly, the jury agreed with them and refused to find either man guilty of anything. Both were immediately set free by the judge, even though they had admitted to planning an illegal escape and then carrying it out.

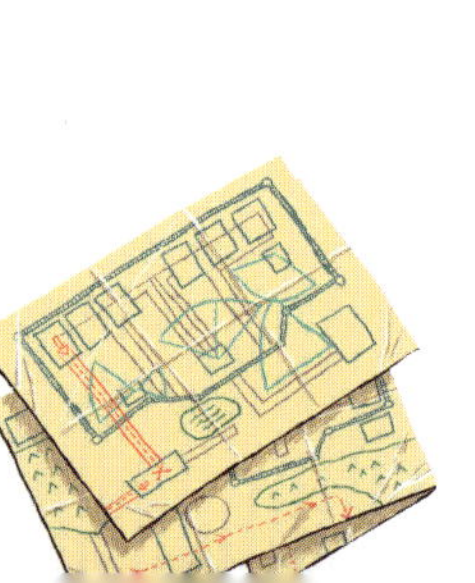

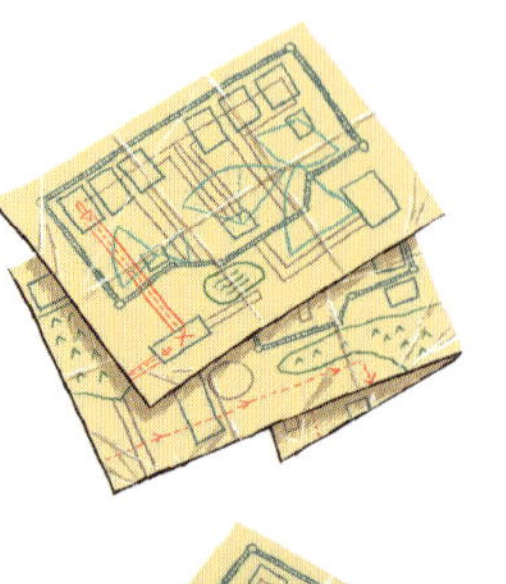

Armando Socarrás Ramírez

Frozen and Alone at 8,000 Metres (Cuba, 1969)

Imagine spending all day curled up in a tiny metal compartment more than eight kilometres above the ground. When Armando Socarrás Ramírez actually did this, he had barely enough air to keep him alive, nothing at all to eat or drink, and at times the temperature plunged far below zero as the world rushed past him at almost 900 kilometres an hour.

Ramírez was only a teenager when he became what airline pilots call a 'wheel-well stowaway'. He and his friend Jorge Pérez Blanco had both been so desperate to escape from the Caribbean island of Cuba that they had decided to try climbing on to a moving jet just seconds before it took off on an international flight out of Cuba.

Life in Cuba was extremely hard for ordinary families like theirs. The island was ruled by a dictator and most of the people living there were very poor and often hungry. Ramírez was already training to become a welder, but this wasn't the job he wanted. He dreamed of being an artist and thought he'd have a better chance of becoming one if he went to live with his uncle in the US.

Ramírez and his friend knew that by trying to escape they were taking a huge gamble. Climbing on to a moving aeroplane would be extremely dangerous, but the pair were so keen get out of Cuba that they were prepared to risk their lives.

In June 1969 the boys headed to the airport in Havana and successfully identified a McDonnell Douglas DC-8 airliner that was heading to Spain. While no one was looking, they clambered on to its wheel struts and then squeezed themselves into two cramped compartments above. The wheels and struts of an aircraft are known as its undercarriage, and this retracts into these compartments after take-off. Several people had already been crushed to death after trying this because the compartments were never designed to hold a human being, while others had lost their grip and fallen out. To stop this happening to him, Ramírez had brought some rope to secure himself to the aircraft, but neither he nor Blanco had any idea if there would be enough space for them in the compartments once the pilot started to raise the undercarriage. Now, as a pair of giant wheels moved towards him, Ramírez was aware of the heat coming off the tyres, which only seconds before had been powering down the runway at nearly 300 kilometres an hour.

Ramírez felt himself being squashed, but not crushed, by the enormous tyres as the compartment doors swung closed, and he assumed the same thing was happening to his

friend on the other side of the aircraft. His relief was immense but very short-lived because, a couple of seconds later, the doors began to open again and the undercarriage started to go back down.

Ramírez was terrified and held on as tightly as he could with his fingertips. Unbeknown to him, the pilots had just seen a red flashing light on the flight deck warning them that the undercarriage had not retracted fully. Fortunately, they tried a second time, and this gave Ramírez a few seconds in which to tie his rope as securely as he could. Once he had checked the knots, he had to hope they would be enough to stop him falling out later on, when the undercarriage was lowered so the aircraft could land at its destination just outside the Spanish capital.

Madrid airport, however, was more than 7,000 kilometres from Cuba, which meant he had to spend at least eight hours curled up in the dark. He had stuffed his ears full of cotton wool, but the sound of the jet's four engines was still deafening. Ramírez had also brought along some painkillers, which he crammed into his mouth and swallowed.

This was the seventeen-year-old's first-ever flight, but his experience could not have been more different to that of the 147 passengers and ten crew in the spacious cabin a couple of metres above his head. Although the compartment's doors were shut tight, it was getting much colder as the DC-8 climbed higher and higher over the ocean. Curled up in the dark, Ramírez soon began to shiver uncontrollably. More than anything, he was wishing he had

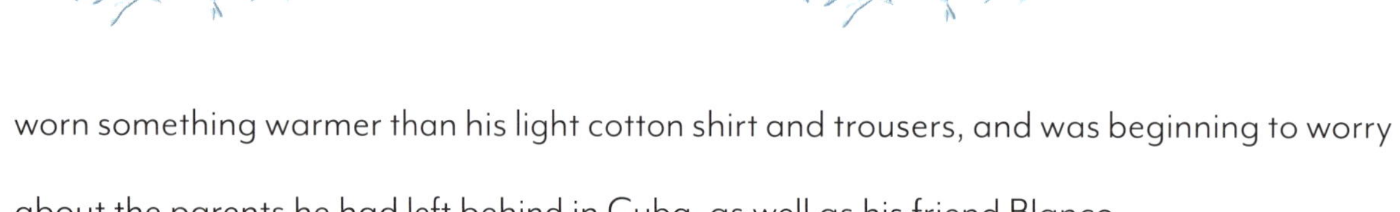

worn something warmer than his light cotton shirt and trousers, and was beginning to worry about the parents he had left behind in Cuba, as well as his friend Blanco.

However, at some point high above the Atlantic, the teenager blacked out, and almost certainly remained unconscious for the rest of the flight. This could have been because he was freezing cold and stressed, or due to the lack of oxygen at high altitude, or possibly both. All we know is that when the DC-8 landed at Madrid's Barajas Airport and came to a standstill outside the terminal building, the body of Armando Socarrás Ramírez dropped out of the wheel well and lay on the concrete. Worryingly, there was no sign at all of Blanco, while Ramírez's body was literally frozen stiff. Layers of ice had built up around his mouth and nose, and it was almost impossible for anyone to tell if he was even breathing.

Although he later claimed to have a vague memory of lying on the ground, Ramírez was certainly unconscious again by the time he was loaded into an ambulance and driven away from the airport. It was many hours before he woke up in a bed in Madrid's main hospital, several days before he was able to get out of bed and walk around, and weeks before he could hear anything that was said to him by anyone else in the ward.

The fact that he survived at all was described by his doctors as a medical miracle. When his temperature was first taken at the hospital, one said it was too low even to register on the thermometer. Aviation experts confirmed that at such a high altitude, the temperature must have fallen as low as –40°C, and an airline engineer explained to journalists that the chance

of someone not being crushed by the retracting undercarriage of a DC-8 was about one in a million.

No one at the hospital could explain how this lucky young man had managed to survive for so long with so little oxygen, nor, indeed, how he was able to recover so completely. Sadly, his friend shared none of his good fortune. Blanco never made it to Spain at all. It was only much later that Ramírez discovered that he had fallen out of his compartment as the aircraft took off from Havana. Blanco was lucky to have survived but was promptly arrested and imprisoned. Because of this he was never able to rejoin his friend, who still lives in the US with his wife and large family.

'Dan Cooper'

Vanishing into Thin Air (US, 1971)

Forcing an aircraft to fly somewhere other than its scheduled destination is a crime known as hijacking or air piracy. It is usually committed by terrorists, either by pointing a gun at the pilot's head or by hiding a bomb somewhere on board. The hijackers may decide to hold the passengers and crew to ransom as a way of publicising their own political demands or threaten to blow up the aircraft unless the authorities agree to release other terrorists from prison.

However, not every hijack happens this way. Sometimes the hijackers are just ordinary criminals, people looking for a way to steal a large sum of money from the government or the airline that owns the hijacked aircraft. This happened in the US in November 1971, when a man calling himself Dan Cooper bought a one-way ticket for a short flight in a Boeing 727 between the cities of Portland and Seattle.

The man boarded the plane and shortly after take-off handed a scribbled note to a member of the cabin crew telling her he was carrying a bomb. He said it was in his black briefcase,

which he opened slightly to show her what looked like sticks of dynamite. Cooper explained that he wanted four parachutes and $200,000 in cash or he would blow up the plane. These were to be loaded on to the jet when it reached Seattle. In exchange for the money, Cooper agreed to release the passengers before the 727 took off again and headed for Mexico.

Mexico is more than 2,000 kilometres south of Seattle, but before the aircraft had travelled even half this distance, the hijacker did something extraordinary. Ordering the flight crew to stay at the front of the aircraft, he put on one of the parachutes, opened the Boeing's rear passenger door, leaped out and was gone. By this time it was dark, and America's most mysterious hijacker was never seen again. Dan Cooper, or whatever his real name was, had simply vanished into thin air – and escaped with a huge amount of money.

By the time the aircraft landed in the US state of Nevada, FBI agents were already busy looking for him. They began by questioning a Seattle resident called D. B. Cooper. He apparently had a criminal record, but they soon established that he couldn't be the hijacker, so a massive nationwide manhunt was authorised to begin straightaway.

The FBI's biggest problem was identifying the place where the hijacker might have landed. The pilots knew the approximate location of the aircraft at the moment when Cooper had made his escape, but a parachute can drift miles in the wind and rarely goes down in a straight line. The FBI decided it needed a spy plane to study the ground below the jet's flight path and help its agents identify the hijacker's drop zone.

The Lockheed SR-71 must have looked ideal for the job. As well as being the world's fastest aeroplane, with a top speed of more than 3,500 kilometres per hour, it was equipped with one of the most advanced cameras ever invented. This combination enabled the crew to photograph hundreds of square kilometres at a time, and to do this in almost microscopic detail. Even flying at twice the height of an ordinary airliner, and at nearly double the speed of a modern fighter jet, the camera was reportedly so sensitive that it could spot an object on the ground that was no larger than a shoe.

Scanning the terrain along the entire route with such a magnificent machine didn't take very long at all, but, frustratingly, nothing useful turned up. The pictures from five separate SR-71 flights revealed no abandoned parachute, no sign of Cooper and none of the missing money.

Next, the FBI experimented by throwing a man-sized load out of the rear door of another 727 to see where it would land. This didn't work either. The heavy package fell close to Mount St Helens, America's deadliest volcano, in an area that was covered in trees. Once again, after a careful search by agents and local police working on foot, nothing significant was found. Two nearby lakes were explored using boats and even a miniature submarine, and the National Guard brought in helicopters and other small aircraft to follow the route of the hijacked aircraft yet again, once more without success.

By April the following year hundreds of professional and civilian volunteers were still involved in the search, but their efforts had produced nothing connected to Cooper's disappearance

or the missing money. The only excitement came with the gruesome discovery of a skeleton in an old barn, but this was quickly shown to be that of a teenage girl, and the public slowly began to lose interest.

After this the trail seemed to go cold and the costly manhunt was gradually wound down, although the FBI refused to close the case completely. Then, in February 1980, an extraordinary discovery by an eight-year-old boy meant that Dan Cooper was suddenly front-page news once again.

Brian Ingram had been building a campfire while on holiday with his family when he found nearly $6,000 buried in the sandy bank of the Columbia River. The family reported Brian's find to police, and FBI agents quickly confirmed that the serial numbers on the notes exactly matched those on the ransom money paid to the hijacker. They knew this because they had carefully recorded the serial numbers before handing the money over. For the same reason, agents also knew that none of the money had been spent in the nearly ten years since Cooper's disappearance. This has always been one of the most curious aspects of his escape, and it has led many to conclude that he was probably killed after jumping from the plane.

His body has never been found, but it's certainly possible that Cooper perished. Parachuting can be dangerous even for experts, and no one knows if the mystery hijacker was a novice or an expert who had done it many times before. It has also been pointed out that heavily

forested areas make for difficult drop zones, and that when he jumped, the mystery passenger had none of the survival gear that a person would need for a long solo hike through a remote and largely uninhabited area.

But, for all that, the truth is we will probably never know who the hijacker really was or what happened to him in the end. His story certainly captured the public's imagination (Brian Ingram later sold fifteen of the notes for an astonishing $37,000), and at least five people subsequently attempted similar hijacks of their own. Interestingly, all five survived the parachute jump, though all were arrested shortly afterwards. Dan Cooper avoided that fate, but perhaps only because his own 'escape' had ended with his death.

Dilip Parulkar

A Knife, a Fork, Scissors and Some Apricots (Pakistan, 1972)

Tens of thousands of troops were killed or injured during thirteen days of bitter fighting in the Indo-Pakistani War of December 1971, and many more were taken prisoner by both sides. The captives included three Indian Air Force pilots who made a daring escape attempt in August 1972.

Dilip Parulkar had already told his commanding officer that he would definitely try to escape if he were ever captured, and he wasted no time in putting a plan into action after his Sukhoi jet was shot down during a mission to destroy an enemy radar station. Parulkar successfully parachuted down to the ground but was captured almost immediately and taken to a prison camp at Rawalpindi. After being interrogated he was locked up in a filthy cell with several of his fellow airmen. Chatting to Melvinder Grewal and Harish Sinhji, it didn't take him long to work out that they were as keen as he was to escape from the prison and get back to India.

All three were convinced that finding a way out of the camp would be the easy part. The real challenge would be travelling hundreds of kilometres, many of them on foot, without being spotted by an enemy patrol or accidentally killed by their own side. They knew they would also have to avoid the local villagers, who had already beaten up a number of Indian pilots whose aircraft had been shot down over Pakistan.

To prepare for their long hike the trio began stocking up on supplies. By using torn curtains, belts and parachute fabric, they made backpacks to carry everything they would need. Prisoners in the camp earned a small allowance each month (equivalent to about 60p), which they could use to buy things from the guards. The three men bought tins of condensed milk, chocolate and dried apricots and stuffed them into the backpacks.

Military pilots have to be skilled navigators, but the men were deep inside what was, to them, unknown territory. To help find a route out of Pakistan they magnetised some needles using the battery from a prison radio and then hid them inside a pen. Magnetised needles always point north, so they planned to use them as compasses to work out which direction to go in once they left the camp. Parulkar also restitched various items of clothing to make them look more like the light cotton garments worn by the people living in and around Rawalpindi.

First, though, they had to get out of the camp. Their initial idea had been to kidnap one of the guards and refuse to let him go until they were all set free. One guard always looked like he was half asleep, and Parulkar was confident they could surprise him one night and steal his revolver. However, after thinking the plan through, he realised the other guards would probably just shoot the three would-be escapees – and then maybe even the guard for being so useless. Clearly, they would have to think of something else, something much less dramatic.

Every prison has strict rules about the things prisoners can have in their cells. Obviously, no tools are allowed, but the three men managed to steal a knife and a fork from the canteen, which they quickly squirrelled away. They also tricked a guard into giving them a pair of scissors, which they did by giving up shaving and then asking for scissors to trim their new beards.

Although these items were small, they were sharp and strong enough to scrape away the *masala* between the bricks in the cell wall. *Masala* is like cement, and by removing some of it the men hoped they could loosen the bricks enough to make a hole. This took time, however, because the prison wall was nearly half a metre thick.

Grewal and Parulkar set to work and spent four or five weeks working away at the *masala* every night until they had a hole big enough to crawl through. Sinhji kept watch while they did this, and during the day one of their beds would be pushed against the wall to hide their handiwork from the guards.

Once the hole was large enough, the three men squeezed through it and found themselves standing in the crowded street outside. Luckily, no one had spotted them coming through

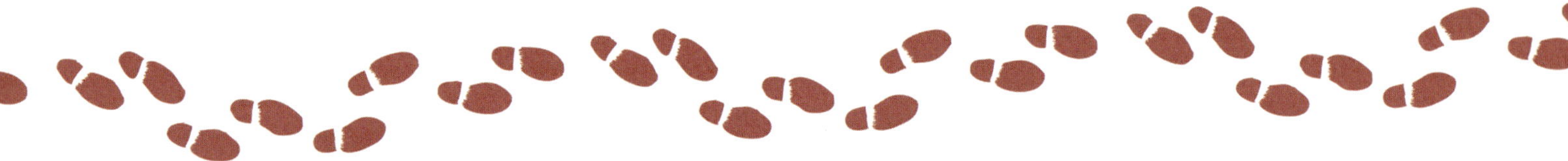

the wall, and keen to get away from the prison as quickly as possible, they immediately set off on their 500-kilometre cross-country hike.

India and Pakistan have been at war with each other so many times that the frontier between the two countries is still one of the most heavily guarded borders on Earth. Crossing it without being seen was almost impossible in the 1970s, so the three prisoners had decided to head for Afghanistan instead. This meant a much longer trek, but before escaping from the prison camp one of them had seen an old map, which showed a quiet railway track that ran in the right direction. If they walked along it, they would arrive at a station called Landi Khana, which was ideal because it was only a few kilometres from the border between Pakistan and Afghanistan.

Unfortunately, when they reached the end of the railway line, they couldn't find the station anywhere, so they had to stop a stranger and ask for directions. It turned out the prison map had been so old that it included a station that no longer existed. Everyone living in this part of Pakistan knew Landi Khana had been shut down forty years before, so the stranger realised that these three men – whoever they were – must be up to something.

An angry crowd quickly gathered, and when someone went to fetch the police, Parulkar and his friends realised they were in trouble. The border was within easy walking distance and they could actually see the mountains of Afghanistan, but they were going nowhere unless they came up with an explanation for why they were there and why they didn't know about Landi Khana.

By the time the police arrived, Parulkar had decided to tell them that he and his friends were Pakistani pilots, not Indian ones. He explained that they were taking a well-earned break from their duties at a nearby airbase, and that none of them had grown up in this part of Pakistan, which is why they didn't know about the station closing. He demanded they be left alone to enjoy their break and warned the police that if they weren't, someone at the airbase would want to know who was causing all this trouble.

Parulkar thought this sounded believable, even the threat at the end, but the police weren't fooled, so the three men were arrested and then carefully searched. When the police found their Indian Air Force identity cards tucked into their clothing, they were taken back to the prison at Rawalpindi and immediately sentenced to thirty days' punishment in solitary confinement.

Having come so far and got so close to freedom and the frontier, being caught in this way was a terrible disappointment. However, their arrest may have been a lucky escape for the men. They knew angry mobs on both sides of the conflict had already beaten and even killed enemy captives, and the police certainly won't have been happy about Parulkar's threats. Given all that, a locked cell in a prison camp was perhaps the safest place for the three to be in. Certainly, they made no more attempts to escape, and after being released from prison the following December, Dilip Parulkar went on to win India's prestigious Vishisht Seva medal.

Gene Hambleton

The Extraordinary Effort to Save a Single Airman (Vietnam, 1972)

When US Air Force colonel Gene Hambleton was shot down over Vietnam in April 1972, his escape from behind enemy lines turned out to be the most complex, most costly one in American military history.

Vietnam was a divided country, and its two halves had already been at war with each other for almost two decades. Communists supported by Russia and China governed the northern half, while the government in the south had the backing of several anti-communist states led by the US.

Hambleton, who used the radio call sign Bat 21 Bravo, had been on his sixty-third mission when his aircraft was hit by a Russian-made missile and exploded. He was the only crew member to survive the blast, but his parachute brought him down in a rice field in one of the most dangerous parts of the country.

The area, Quảng Trị, had been overrun by 30,000 heavily armed enemy troops in what became known as Vietnam's Red Fiery Summer. The US military always made strenuous efforts to rescue lost airmen, and helping Hambleton to escape from Quảng Trị now became its top priority. Bat 21 Bravo's mission had involved spying on the North Vietnamese, and as the senior navigator Hambleton knew far too many secrets for the Americans to risk him being caught and interrogated.

Hambleton had been injured in the explosion, but he carried a small emergency radio with him as he ran to hide in some nearby trees. He'd done some survival training in the past, as well as learning escape and evasion techniques at a specialist jungle school in the Philippines. He knew his job now was to remain hidden and stay alive while a combat search-and-rescue team looked for a way to get him out as quickly as possible.

The team's first attempts to do this went disastrously wrong, however. The injured airman had to watch in horror as five more aircraft were shot down. Another thirteen American personnel were killed or captured trying to reach him and at least nine other planes and helicopters badly damaged, before a senior officer finally called a halt. Quảng Trị was simply too dangerous to risk the lives of any more pilots.

The Americans knew the North Vietnamese listened in to their radio transmissions, so they sent Hambleton a coded message to tell him any further attempts would have to be made by water. He was instructed to make his way to the Cam Lộ river, where he would be met by a US special forces officer called Tom Norris and a small squad of South Vietnamese navy commandos.

Hambleton was already quite close to the river, but reaching it was much tougher than it sounded. After hiding out alone for eight days, he was exhausted, mentally and physically, and nearing the point of starvation. He had lost almost 20 kilogrammes in weight, and to reach the river he had to keep his wits about him and avoid villages that had been occupied by North Vietnamese troops.

Once he reached the Cam Lộ his instructions were to swim east until he met Norris coming the other way, but once he entered the water he realised he no longer had the strength to swim. On the ninth day he actually collapsed on the shore, meaning Norris would have to travel even deeper into enemy territory to find him, revive him and bring him back. The South Vietnamese refused to go along. To them it looked like a suicide mission, and when Norris asked for volunteers, only one of the commandos, Nguyễn Văn Kiệt, raised his hand.

Norris and Kiệt set out on foot, and like Hambleton, they then had to dodge numerous enemy patrols. After a while they came to a deserted, bombed-out village, where they found some old clothes and an abandoned sampan, which is a sort of small canoe. The clothes provided useful disguises, but even dressed as a pair of local fishermen, they knew they had a treacherous journey ahead of them.

As the pair silently rowed upriver, they could see hundreds of North Vietnamese soldiers and even tanks parked along the shore. After several hours Kiệt spotted a body on the south bank, which he guessed must be Hambleton. When they reached him, the airman was still alive but he was in terrible shape. They carefully lifted him into the sampan and hid him beneath bamboo branches, before continuing their slow, silent journey downstream.

It wasn't long before they were spotted by one of the North Vietnamese patrols. The soldiers didn't shoot, so the two men's disguises must have been working, but when Hambleton suddenly woke up and started to say something, Kiệt had to put a hand over his mouth to keep him quiet.

The next time they were spotted they weren't so lucky. Rounding a bend they came face to face with a much larger patrol, whose members immediately started shooting at them. They knew they couldn't afford to return fire because they were so outnumbered, so they paddled as fast as possible to the opposite bank. Kiệt and Norris manhandled Hambleton out of the sampan and turned it over so they could take cover underneath it, before eventually the patrol came under attack from US fighter aircraft and was quickly wiped out.

Pushing the sampan back into the water, the trio continued down the Cam Lộ once again but soon came under attack several more times. Each time they had to duck down into the tiny boat to avoid being struck by small-arms fire, as well as explosive rockets. It was only when they spotted a South Vietnamese armoured personnel carrier on the bank that they realised they were safe at last.

The vehicle had been sent to take them back to a former US Marine base at Đông Hà. From there Hambleton was airlifted to a military hospital. He made a complete recovery, but it was many weeks before he was well again. For their astonishing courage, Tom Norris was awarded the Medal of Honor and Nguyễn Văn Kiệt the US Navy Cross. Kiệt was the only South Vietnamese sailor to receive this prestigious award during a war that lasted almost twenty years.

Colin Armstrong

The One That Got Away (Iraq, 1991)

When Iraq suddenly invaded its neighbour Kuwait in 1990, Britain was one of several countries that sent troops to the region in what became known as Operation Desert Storm.

The British troops included soldiers from the Special Air Service, or SAS, a secretive special forces unit whose members are specially trained to operate behind enemy lines. Their work involves spying on the enemy, as well as carrying out missions to destroy equipment and sabotage military bases in order to prevent hostile forces from fighting effectively.

Naturally, this kind of work is highly dangerous. The lives of SAS soldiers are often put at risk, and in January 1991 several of them were forced to abandon a mission after it went very badly wrong. The soldiers were part of a small, eight-man patrol that had been sent into enemy territory to disrupt the activities of the Iraqi army and locate its mobile missile launchers.

Their problems started almost as soon as a low-flying Chinook helicopter had dropped them into the combat zone. One of the men realised his radio equipment was broken, and shortly afterwards several others were spotted by a Bedouin tribesman out looking for his goats. The broken radio made it impossible to communicate properly with SAS headquarters, and being seen by the Bedouin lost them the element of surprise that is a vital part of almost every SAS patrol.

The team knew this man would give away their position to a local army commander, so they decided to abandon the mission. This meant they had to 'exfiltrate' – meaning clear out of the area – as quickly as possible. Exfiltration usually involves abandoning equipment (or destroying it to stop it falling into enemy hands) and then being airlifted to safety under cover of darkness. Unfortunately, the helicopter pilot was unable to reach them, and all their attempts to communicate with other friendly aircraft in that part of Iraq were unsuccessful.

When the patrol was fired on by Iraqi forces, the men broke up and became separated. Six were captured almost immediately or died trying to reach a safe place. Another was arrested by the Iraqis after trying to steal a vehicle, which he hoped to use to escape. In the end only one man got away, and that was the patrol's medic, Colin Armstrong.

Armstrong had decided that his best chance was to head north towards Iraq's border with Syria. Soldiers in the SAS undergo months of rigorous escape and evasion training, but Armstrong's plan involved the added danger of heading even deeper into enemy territory. His escape would require him to stay out of sight for more than a week as he made his way towards the border, which was at least 300 kilometres away.

Even before abandoning the mission, Armstrong had been worried about his equipment. He had spent time in Siberia, the high Alps and even on Everest, and he knew that the clothing he'd been issued with was not suitable for nights in the freezing rain and snow of the Iraqi desert. On top of that, not only did he have no food supplies or water, he also had to rely on a compass that didn't work properly and SAS maps that were out of date.

Moving only at night in order to stay hidden, Armstrong was at least able to use the position of the Moon and stars to navigate. He knew he would eventually reach Syria if he kept travelling northwards, but he had no idea how long this would take. At this point there was no way of knowing who or what he might encounter along the way either, although he did discover much later on that more than 1,500 Iraqi troops had been trying to track him down, as well as hundreds of ordinary Iraqi citizens.

From his survival training Armstrong recognised that many of the symptoms he was beginning to experience were signs that he was becoming exhausted and dangerously dehydrated. As the days wore on, his symptoms included feeling dizzy and losing his sense of direction, sudden mood swings, confusion and drowsiness. More than once Armstrong wondered whether he would survive the next day, but he knew he had only two choices: he could either keep going or just lie down and die.

It took him several days to reach the Euphrates river. This flows down from Syria, so it was confirmation that he was still heading in the right direction. A major river like the Euphrates should have been easy to follow, except that river banks are often busy places, which made it even more difficult for Armstrong to stay out of sight.

Nevertheless, he carefully followed the river for the next three days, moving mostly at night and spending the daylight hours in ditches and drainage tunnels to stay out of sight. At last, just when he thought he could walk no further, he spotted the border town of Krabilah. He assumed this meant he had made it to safety at last, but unfortunately he was mistaken: what he saw was a different town altogether. Syria was still several kilometres away, and when he realised this he felt crushed. Completely worn out, he collapsed and broke his nose after falling face first into a wall.

How he found the mental and physical strength to get up again is impossible to explain. His boots were as broken as his nose, both feet were bleeding and raw, and he was delirious from a lack of food and water. On the morning of his eighth day on the run he saw an isolated building a few hundred metres away and decided that he would kill the occupants, if that was what it took to get a drink of fresh water.

In the event, there was no need. The building was manned by some cheerful Syrian border guards, who gave him water and lots of strong, sweet tea. After the Syrian police had established that he was who he said he was, Armstrong was released and driven to the British Embassy.

The physical impact of his eight-day ordeal had been enormous, and perhaps unsurprisingly, Armstrong never returned to operational duties. He remained in the SAS for another three years, however, and still holds the record for the longest escape and evasion mission ever undertaken by a member of Britain's elite special forces regiment.

Phil Ashby

Attacked and Unarmed (Sierra Leone, 2000)

Most countries today belong to the United Nations, an organisation set up nearly eighty years ago to promote peace and reduce poverty and suffering in the world's poorest regions. As part of its peacekeeping role, the UN sends huge numbers of men and women called 'observers' into conflict zones every year. These people are unarmed, and their job is to search for peaceful solutions when countries are at war.

As observers they don't fight, but because they don't support either side in a war, they often come under attack from both. This makes the peacekeeping process extremely dangerous, which is one of the reasons why so many UN staff are ex-military. Major Phil Ashby is a good example of this, a young Royal Marines officer who volunteered to join the UN in the West African state of Sierra Leone. His work there involved encouraging members of a rebel army called the Revolutionary United Front (RUF) to stop fighting and surrender their weapons.

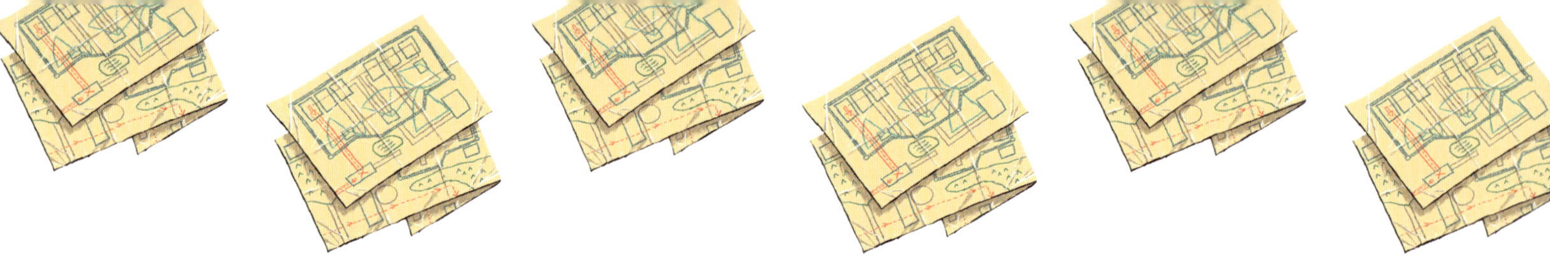

In April 2000 Ashby and his colleagues helped set up an official disarmament camp at Makeni, in the middle of the rebels' territory. By the start of May only a handful of rebels had been persuaded to hand in their weapons, but even though it was a tiny number, the rebel leaders were infuriated. Accusing the UN of stealing their weapons, hundreds of RUF members launched a violent attack on Ashby and his fellow volunteers.

Many of the attackers were young boy-soldiers, often only eleven or twelve years old. Some were as young as five, but they were armed with Russian AK-47 assault rifles and heavily outnumbered the UN staff inside the camp, making its defence impossible. Several peacekeepers were killed in the attack, while others were taken hostage and tortured. The survivors were convinced that they would be murdered if they didn't escape, and so on 5 May Ashby and his comrades scaled the camp's high back wall in the dead of night. The three Britons and a New Zealander then fled into the surrounding jungle as the rebels moved in to burn the camp to the ground.

No one had planned for this, so they left Makeni with very few supplies. The men carried a little shortwave radio with them, as well as a satellite telephone, a map and a compass. The only food they could find was a loaf of bread, some baked beans and a few army rations. Each man also had a litre of water with him, but this wouldn't last long at all in the heat of a tropical rainforest.

Two of them were still recovering from a serious bout of illness that had left them much weaker than usual. Another major problem was that the satellite phone was almost out of

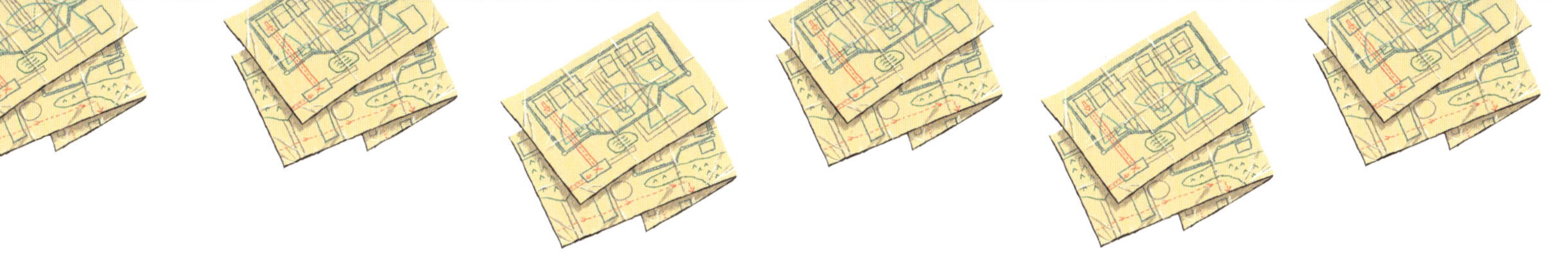

power. Ashby used it to quickly telephone his wife, who then told the authorities in London that the men were trying to escape. But after that the phone went dead, leaving them with no way to communicate with the outside world.

They found the radio was useful for hearing the news and the football scores. However, what the four really needed was a way of calling for help. With the fighting getting worse every day, the RUF had soon captured another 500 UN personnel.

Makeni was in the north of the rebel-held territory, so Ashby decided their best hope was to head south as fast as possible. They hoped to reach another UN base about 60 kilometres away at Magburaka, but it was clear that what had started as an attack on their small camp had now erupted into a full-scale civil war.

The RUF was becoming increasingly violent and increasingly anti-British, which made travelling through the jungle a lot more difficult. More than ever, the men knew they really stood out from the locals. All were fair-skinned and, especially in Ashby's case, unusually tall. From now on they would have to assume that anyone they encountered in the jungle was a possible RUF killer. In practice, this meant avoiding everyone, and the best way to do this was to hide out during the day and walk at night. The only places to hide were among the poisonous ants and snakes in the undergrowth, and for a while it seemed as if what kept the men going was their heightened sense of danger and the adrenaline pumping round their bodies.

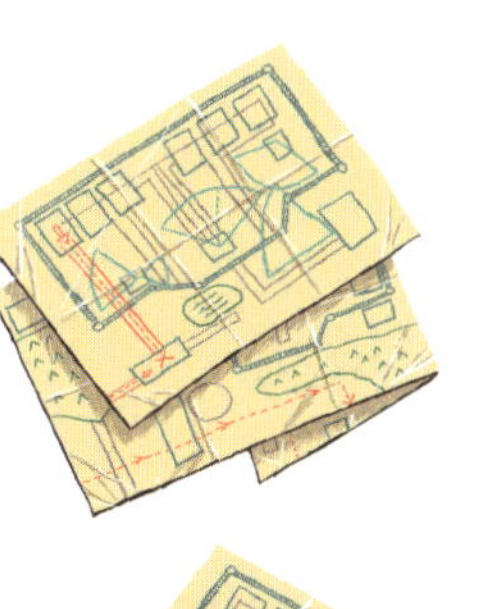

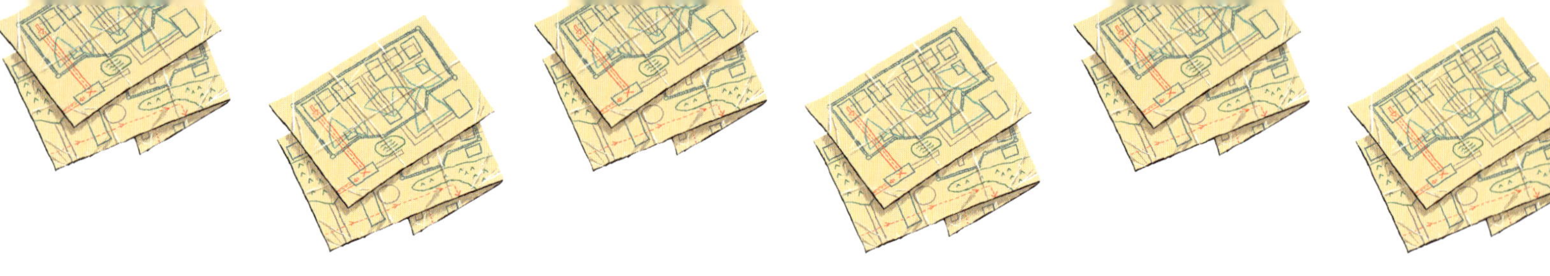

Their discomfort was constant, however, and it must have been hard not to panic or give up. The hot, thick air buzzed day and night with the sound of a million stinging, biting bugs, and with only a litre each, it didn't take long for the water to run out. Once this happened they struggled to find anything at all to drink. May was in the middle of the region's dry season, and each time they reached one of the rivers marked on their map it turned out to be no more than a few shrinking pools of stagnant, undrinkable slime littered with dead insects.

The upside to this was that the men's severe thirst stopped them from realising how hungry they were. But the downside was much more obvious: if they didn't reach a source of fresh water pretty soon, none of them would survive another day in the rainforest. Eventually, they had to resort to drinking their own urine, a desperate, horrible measure that no doctor would ever recommend.

Despite these hardships they kept going for almost a week through some of Africa's toughest and most dangerous jungle terrain. As they got closer to Magburaka, however, the men had an extraordinary stroke of luck when they ran into a local teenager who had also suffered at the hands of the RUF. Because of this, he recognised the peacekeepers as friends and offered to help them. He was able to guide them the last few hundred metres to a safe UN area, and once there Ashby was able to recharge his telephone. Within minutes, a helicopter was on its way to get the men out, and their escape was complete.

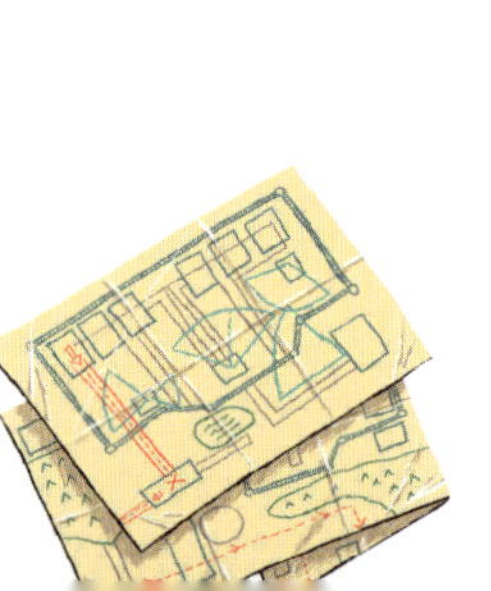

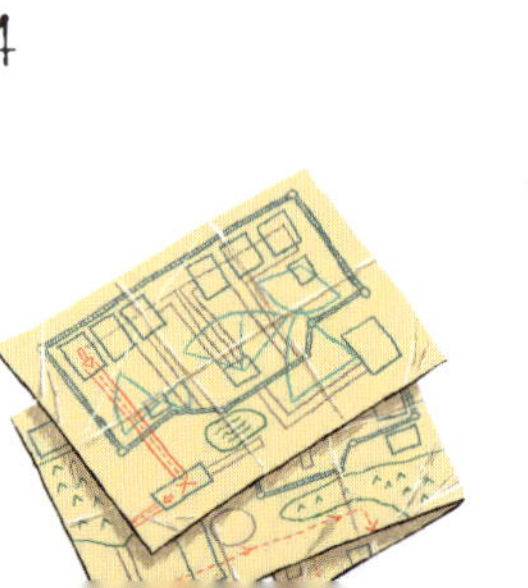

Susan LeFevre

Learning to Behave (US, 2008)

In 2008 Marie Walsh was living happily in San Diego, California. She had a husband she loved, three children and a large, comfortable home. She played tennis regularly and enjoyed gardening, and was weeding the flower beds in her front garden when some armed US marshals turned up with an arrest warrant for a woman called Susan LeFevre.

Susan LeFevre was a name she hadn't heard for more than thirty years. It wasn't a name anyone in the neighbourhood knew, and it certainly wasn't the one Marie used when she signed birthday cards and letters to her San Diego friends. It was a name that Marie knew very well, though, because Susan LeFevre was the name she'd been born with and the one she had used prior to escaping from prison in the 1970s.

In 1974 Susan LeFevre was only nineteen years old when she and a friend were arrested for trying to sell a couple of grammes of illegal drugs to an undercover police officer. After being tried and found guilty, they were each sentenced to between ten and twenty years in prison, which was an unusually long sentence for a first offence involving such a small quantity of an illegal substance.

Fortunately, the prison in Michigan that LeFevre was sent to wasn't a high-security one, and a year or so into her sentence she managed to climb over a high barbed-wire fence without being seen. She dropped down on the other side and ran to a nearby street, where she had secretly arranged to meet her grandfather in his parked car.

The pair immediately drove a few miles from the prison, but LeFevre knew that she had to get much further away if she was to avoid being caught. Because she couldn't risk going back home, her grandfather had brought some clean clothes and a toothbrush with him, as well as a couple of hundred dollars from her mother to help her on her way.

The money was very welcome but it wasn't a lot, so LeFevre decided the best thing to do would be to hitch a ride out of Michigan with friends instead of travelling on public transport. She was lucky that they were happy to help her, and she was able to travel several thousand kilometres across America without arousing suspicion or being spotted by the police.

Before arriving in California she had decided on a change of identity, and by the time she met her future husband she had got used to calling herself Marie, which was actually her middle name. She kept up the pretence when they got married a few years later and made sure no one knew what she was really called or what she had done all those years ago.

When the marshals knocked on her door more than thirty years later, the mother-of-three knew she could be sent back to prison, and because she had escaped, might even have to serve an extra five years on top of the original sentence. But she also realised that she couldn't go on pretending to be someone else forever. When one of the marshals asked her if she really was called Susan LeFevre, she admitted she was, and she made no attempt to run away when he told her that she was under arrest.

Instead, LeFevre decided to ask the court for mercy. She argued that she'd been very young at the time of her offence and that the drugs were for her and her friend's use, meaning she wasn't really a drug dealer. She also said she'd only pleaded guilty in the original trial because her lawyer had told her she'd get a short sentence if she did. Afterwards she'd been horrified by its length, and that was the main reason she had decided to escape.

Now, in 2008, she had a different lawyer, who asked for the case to be thrown out of court altogether. The judge refused to do this, pointing out that the drugs she had were illegal, no matter how small the quantity. However, he was clearly impressed by LeFevre herself and by the fact that she'd lived an honest life since reaching California, so he sent her back to prison for little more than a year.

This time she made no attempt to escape, and when a prison committee met to vote on whether or not to release her early, they had little hesitation in letting her go. This made perfect sense. Prison authorities always insist that they want inmates to live good, honest lives when they get out of jail, and that's what Susan LeFevre had done. Admittedly, she had got out illegally in the 1970s – and several years earlier than expected – but she'd gone on to lead an honest life in California and had been careful not to commit any other crimes.

Nadia Murad

Twenty-First-Century Slavery (Iraq, 2014)

ISIS, the Islamic State of Iraq and Syria, is an illegal terrorist organisation that has spent years fighting in parts of the Middle East. It's become notorious for the brutality of its members, who have tortured and killed tens of thousands of ordinary men, women and children.

In 2014 masked ISIS fighters attacked an Iraqi village called Kocho and took the entire population captive. The villagers were Yazidis, members of an ancient ethno-religious group, and they were ordered to convert to Islam or die. Around 800 men who refused were immediately murdered in the most violent ways imaginable, and most of the women and children were taken as ISIS slaves.

Nadia Murad was still a student when she was captured by ISIS. She was forced to witness the murders of more than 300 Yazidi men in a single hour, including six of her eleven older brothers. Later she was taken with a group of other women and girls to the nearby city of Mosul, which had also been overrun by ISIS gangs.

For several weeks the terrified captives were held in small locked rooms, where they were beaten repeatedly, burned with cigarettes and physically abused. Several of the women killed themselves, or tried to, and although Murad never considered doing this, she has said there were times when she wished her captors would just kill her and end her horrific ordeal.

Eventually, the women were taken from their rooms and given or even sold to ISIS fighters as 'wives'. In accordance with ISIS beliefs, Murad became the property of one of the fighters. He took her home and introduced her to his parents, but he was just as vicious as the other ISIS members she had seen. He and his friends treated her appallingly, and he physically attacked her at night.

By November, four months after the Kocho massacre, Murad had been passed around from 'owner' to 'owner' and was desperate to escape. She had been beaten up more times than she could count, but there seemed no way to get away from her captor, until one day he made a simple but important mistake.

Murad was always locked in the man's house whenever he went out. However, that day, after hearing him leave, she realised she hadn't heard the sound of his key turning in the door. Realising her kidnapper had forgotten to lock up the house, Murad ran out into the street and began to look for someone who might help her.

ISIS fighters like to dress in black, so Murad knew she had to find someone who looked like an ordinary Iraqi citizen rather than another one of them. After wandering the streets for several hours, she spotted a man called Omar Abdel Jabar. When she explained who she was, he nervously pulled her into his house and agreed to keep her hidden until she could get out of Mosul.

Helping Murad like this was an incredibly courageous thing for anyone to do. The people of Mosul knew that ISIS offered generous rewards for recaptured slaves but would severely punish anyone caught hiding one or helping them to escape. Jabar was aware of this too, but he had a plan to smuggle Murad out of Mosul using a forged identity card made by his cousin. The false name on the document made it appear as though he and Murad were a married couple. They both hoped this story would be enough to fool the guards at the various ISIS security checkpoints on the roads out of Mosul.

The pair left Mosul by taxi and had to force themselves not to panic each time they came to a checkpoint. One guard after another snatched the identity card away from them and studied it closely. These men were all armed, pointing their weapons into the car as they questioned its occupants. Where was the taxi going? How long had Murad and Jabar been married? What time would they be coming back to Mosul?

Each new checkpoint made Murad and Jabar more nervous than the last, but eventually they came to the final one and passed through it after the usual interrogation. The taxi driver

stopped a few hundred metres away and let them out, and Murad made her way to the safety of a Yazidi refugee camp, well away from the area controlled by ISIS.

As a young girl Nadia Murad had dreamed of becoming a hairdresser or maybe even a teacher, but her experiences in Kocho and Mosul had changed her. Now she was determined to do something to prevent other people from suffering as she had done. She began by telling her story, raising awareness of the dangers that Yazidis and other minorities face around the world. A couple of years later she founded a charity called Nadia's Initiative in order to represent the victims of massacres, human trafficking and other atrocities, and in 2018 this extraordinary young woman became the first Iraqi to be awarded the Nobel Peace Prize. She is still one of its youngest-ever recipients, and the only Yazidi.

Epilogue

Real-life escape stories like the ones in this book can be exciting, intriguing, inspiring – or just terrifying. Many of them read like adventure stories, even though they describe events that really happened, and more than a few have been turned into best-selling books and thrilling films featuring some of Hollywood's biggest stars.

It's easy to feel positive about many of them: for example, the stories explaining how dozens of brave men and women managed to escape from prison camps during World Wars I and II. Even those who were our enemies at the time were heroes to their own side, and a lot of these wartime prisoners saw risking their lives in an attempt to escape as an important part of doing their patriotic duty.

But in peacetime it's a lot more complicated. Some of the most daring escapes from ordinary jails have involved digging lengthy home-made tunnels under walls, flying remote-control drones into prison yards and even stealing helicopters and private planes. Unfortunately, elaborate escapes like these tend to involve the worst, most violent criminals. We might admire the ingenuity they showed or their sheer determination to get out of prison no matter what, but it's important not to glamorise them. These people aren't like prisoners of war at all. They usually deserve to be in jail, sometimes to serve long sentences. None of us wants to hear on the news that a murderer or an armed robber has escaped and is back out on the streets, no matter how clever the escape plan seemed to be and how long it took to organise.

That's something to think about when we read that the three men who escaped from Alcatraz (see p. 149) were never caught. They could be congratulated for having got away with it – assuming they didn't drown and weren't eaten by sharks – except that they were tried and convicted for very serious crimes. But then again, Alcatraz had a reputation as one of the worst prisons in the US, so perhaps no one should be surprised that they wanted to get free.

George Blake's remarkable escape from Wormwood Scrubs in London is similar (see p. 155). His sentence was unusually long, and the jury refused to convict the men who helped him escape, even though they admitted they had done so. On the other hand, Blake himself admitted that he had betrayed at least 400 of his friends and fellow agents – and we know that in many cases this led directly to them being killed.

In other words, real-life escape stories may be exciting, but they're also highly complicated. Not everyone who manages to escape deserves their freedom as much as Henry 'Box' Brown did in 1849, or should be treated as a hero like Lillian Gutteridge was almost a hundred years later and Nadia Murad is today.

ABOUT THE AUTHOR

Writer and historian David Long is the award-winning and bestselling author of the acclaimed Survivors series, *Pirates Magnified*, *We are the Romans*, *The World's Most Magnificent Machines*, *Tragedy at Sea*, *The Story of the London Underground* and more than twenty other non-fiction books on a wide range of historical subjects. He is married to Rosy and lives in Suffolk.

ABOUT THE ILLUSTRATOR

Jamie Coe is a London-based illustrator, comic-book artist and storyboard artist. After graduating from Central Saint Martins, Jamie's debut graphic novel *Art Schooled* was published by Nobrow Press. Over the years, he's illustrated for many exciting clients, including *The New Yorker*, BBC, DC Comics, Scholastic, *GQ*, *The Telegraph*, Manchester United, *The Atlantic* and Birds Eye.